Getting started with

UNIX

A widely used multiuser operating system

THE ULTIMATE BEGINNERS GUIDE

Table of Contents

UNIX / LINUX Tutorial

Unix is a computer Operating System which is capable of handling activities from multiple users at the same time. The development of Unix started around 1969 at AT&T Bell Labs by Ken Thompson and Dennis Ritchie. This tutorial gives a very good understanding on Unix.

Audience

This tutorial has been prepared for the beginners to help them understand the basics to advanced concepts covering Unix commands, Unix shell scripting and various utilities.

Prerequisites

We assume you have adequate exposure to Operating Systems and their functionalities. A basic understanding on various computer concepts will also help you in understanding the various exercises given in this tutorial.

Unix - Getting Started

What is Unix ?

The Unix operating system is a set of programs that act as a link between the computer and the user.

The computer programs that allocate the system resources and coordinate all the details of the computer's internals is called the operating system or the kernel.

Users communicate with the kernel through a program known as the shell. The shell is a command line interpreter; it translates commands entered by the user and converts them into a language that is understood by the kernel.

- Unix was originally developed in 1969 by a group of AT&T employees Ken Thompson, Dennis Ritchie, Douglas McIlroy, and Joe Ossanna at Bell Labs.
- There are various Unix variants available in the market. Solaris Unix, AIX, HP Unix and BSD are a few examples. Linux is also a flavor of Unix which is freely available.
- Several people can use a Unix computer at the same time; hence Unix is called a multiuser system.
- A user can also run multiple programs at the same time; hence Unix is a multitasking environment.

Unix Architecture

Here is a basic block diagram of a Unix system –

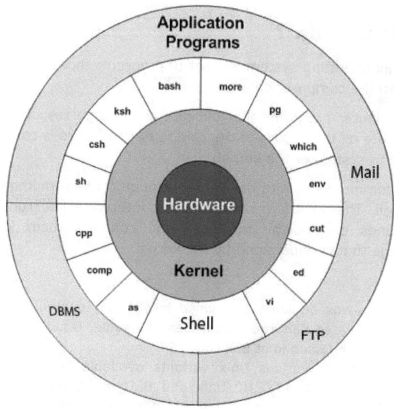

The main concept that unites all the versions of Unix is the following four basics –

- Kernel – The kernel is the heart of the operating system. It interacts with the hardware and most of the tasks like memory management, task scheduling and file management.
- Shell – The shell is the utility that processes your requests. When you type in a command at your terminal, the shell interprets the command and calls the program that you want. The shell uses standard syntax for all commands. C

Shell, Bourne Shell and Korn Shell are the most famous shells which are available with most of the Unix variants.

- Commands and Utilities − There are various commands and utilities which you can make use of in your day to day activities. cp, mv, catand grep, etc. are few examples of commands and utilities. There are over 250 standard commands plus numerous others provided through 3rd party software. All the commands come along with various options.
- Files and Directories − All the data of Unix is organized into files. All files are then organized into directories. These directories are further organized into a tree-like structure called the filesystem.

System Bootup

If you have a computer which has the Unix operating system installed in it, then you simply need to turn on the system to make it live.

As soon as you turn on the system, it starts booting up and finally it prompts you to log into the system, which is an activity to log into the system and use it for your day-to-day activities.

Login Unix

When you first connect to a Unix system, you usually see a prompt such as the following −

login:

To log in

- Have your userid (user identification) and password ready. Contact your system administrator if you don't have these yet.

- Type your userid at the login prompt, then press ENTER. Your userid is case-sensitive, so be sure you type it exactly as your system administrator has instructed.
- Type your password at the password prompt, then press ENTER. Your password is also case-sensitive.
- If you provide the correct userid and password, then you will be allowed to enter into the system. Read the information and messages that comes up on the screen, which is as follows.

```
login : amrood
amrood's password:
Last login: Sun Jun 14 09:32:32 2009 from 62.61.164.73
$
```

You will be provided with a command prompt (sometime called the $ prompt) where you type all your commands. For example, to check calendar, you need to type the cal command as follows –

```
$ cal
     June 2009
Su Mo Tu We Th Fr Sa
    1  2  3  4  5  6
 7  8  9 10 11 12 13
14 15 16 17 18 19 20
21 22 23 24 25 26 27
28 29 30

$
```

Change Password

All Unix systems require passwords to help ensure that your files and data remain your own and that the system itself is secure from hackers and crackers. Following are the steps to change your password —

Step 1 — To start, type password at the command prompt as shown below.

Step 2 — Enter your old password, the one you're currently using.

Step 3 — Type in your new password. Always keep your password complex enough so that nobody can guess it. But make sure, you remember it.

Step 4 — You must verify the password by typing it again.

```
$ passwd
Changing password for amrood
(current) Unix password:******
New UNIX password:*******
Retype new UNIX password:*******
passwd: all authentication tokens updated  successfully

$
```

Note — We have added asterisk (*) here just to show the location where you need to enter the current and new passwords otherwise at your system. It does not show you any character when you type.

Listing Directories and Files

All data in Unix is organized into files. All files are organized into directories. These directories are organized into a tree-like structure called the filesystem.

You can use the ls command to list out all the files or directories available in a directory. Following is the example of using ls command with -l option.

```
$ ls -l
total 19621
drwxrwxr-x  2 amrood amrood     4096 Dec 25 09:59 uml
-rw-rw-r--  1 amrood amrood     5341 Dec 25 08:38 uml.jpg
drwxr-xr-x  2 amrood amrood     4096 Feb 15 2006 univ
drwxr-xr-x  2 root   root       4096 Dec 9  2007 urlspedia
-rw-r--r--  1 root   root     276480 Dec 9  2007 urlspedia.tar
drwxr-xr-x  8 root   root       4096 Nov 25 2007 usr
-rwxr-xr-x  1 root   root       3192 Nov 25 2007 webthumb.php
-rw-rw-r--  1 amrood amrood    20480 Nov 25 2007 webthumb.tar
-rw-rw-r--  1 amrood amrood     5654 Aug 9  2007 yourfile.mid
-rw-rw-r--  1 amrood amrood   166255 Aug 9  2007 yourfile.swf

$
```

Here entries starting with d..... represent directories. For example, uml, univ and urlspedia are directories and rest of the entries are files.

Who Are You?

While you're logged into the system, you might be willing to know : Who am I?

The easiest way to find out "who you are" is to enter the whoami command –

```
$ whoami
amrood
$
```

Try it on your system. This command lists the account name associated with the current login. You can try who am i command as well to get information about yourself.

Who is Logged in?

Sometime you might be interested to know who is logged in to the computer at the same time.

There are three commands available to get you this information, based on how much you wish to know about the other users: users, who, and w.

```
$ users
amrood bablu qadir

$ who
amrood ttyp0 Oct 8 14:10 (limbo)
bablu  ttyp2 Oct 4 09:08 (calliope)
qadir ttyp4 Oct 8 12:09 (dent)

$
```

Try the w command on your system to check the output. This lists down information associated with the users logged in the system.

Logging Out

When you finish your session, you need to log out of the system. This is to ensure that nobody else accesses your files.

To log out

- Just type the logout command at the command prompt, and the system will clean up everything and break the connection.

System Shutdown

The most consistent way to shut down a Unix system properly via the command line is to use one of the following commands –

S.No.	Command & Description
1	**halt** Brings the system down immediately
2	**init 0** Powers off the system using predefined scripts to synchronize and clean up the system prior to shutting down

3	**init 6** Reboots the system by shutting it down completely and then restarting it
4	**poweroff** Shuts down the system by powering off
5	**reboot** Reboots the system
6	**shutdown** Shuts down the system

You typically need to be the super user or root (the most privileged account on a Unix system) to shut down the system. However, on some standalone or personally-owned Unix boxes, an administrative user and sometimes regular users can do so.

Unix - File Management

In this chapter, we will discuss in detail about file management in Unix. All data in Unix is organized into files. All files are organized into directories. These directories are organized into a tree-like structure called the filesystem.

When you work with Unix, one way or another, you spend most of your time working with files. This tutorial will help you understand how to create and remove files, copy and rename them, create links to them, etc.

In Unix, there are three basic types of files —

- Ordinary Files — An ordinary file is a file on the system that contains data, text, or program instructions. In this tutorial, you look at working with ordinary files.
- Directories — Directories store both special and ordinary files. For users familiar with Windows or Mac OS, Unix directories are equivalent to folders.
- Special Files — Some special files provide access to hardware such as hard drives, CD-ROM drives, modems, and Ethernet adapters. Other special files are similar to aliases or shortcuts and enable you to access a single file using different names.

Listing Files

To list the files and directories stored in the current directory, use the following command —

$ls

Here is the sample output of the above command —

$ls

```
bin       hosts lib    res.03
ch07      hw1   pub    test_results
ch07.bak  hw2   res.01 users
docs      hw3   res.02 work
```

The command ls supports the -l option which would help you to get more information about the listed files —

```
$ls -l
total 1962188

drwxrwxr-x  2 amrood amrood    4096 Dec 25 09:59 uml
-rw-rw-r--  1 amrood amrood    5341 Dec 25 08:38 uml.jpg
drwxr-xr-x  2 amrood amrood    4096 Feb 15  2006 univ
drwxr-xr-x  2 root   root      4096 Dec 9  2007 urlspedia
-rw-r--r--  1 root   root    276480 Dec 9  2007 urlspedia.tar
drwxr-xr-x  8 root   root      4096 Nov 25  2007 usr
drwxr-xr-x  2  200    300      4096 Nov 25  2007 webthumb-1.01
-rwxr-xr-x  1 root   root      3192 Nov 25  2007 webthumb.php
-rw-rw-r--  1 amrood amrood   20480 Nov 25  2007 webthumb.tar
-rw-rw-r--  1 amrood amrood    5654 Aug 9  2007 yourfile.mid
-rw-rw-r--  1 amrood amrood  166255 Aug 9  2007 yourfile.swf
drwxr-xr-x 11 amrood amrood    4096 May 29  2007 zlib-1.2.3
$
```

Here is the information about all the listed columns —

- First Column — Represents the file type and the permission given on the file. Below is the description of all type of files.
- Second Column — Represents the number of memory blocks taken by the file or directory.
- Third Column — Represents the owner of the file. This is the Unix user who created this file.
- Fourth Column — Represents the group of the owner. Every Unix user will have an associated group.

- Fifth Column − Represents the file size in bytes.
- Sixth Column − Represents the date and the time when this file was created or modified for the last time.
- Seventh Column − Represents the file or the directory name.

In the ls -l listing example, every file line begins with a d, -, or l. These characters indicate the type of the file that's listed.

S.No.	Prefix & Description
1	- Regular file, such as an ASCII text file, binary executable, or hard link.
2	**b** Block special file. Block input/output device file such as a physical hard drive.
3	**c** Character special file. Raw input/output device file such as a physical hard drive.

4	d
	Directory file that contains a listing of other files and directories.
5	l
	Symbolic link file. Links on any regular file.
6	p
	Named pipe. A mechanism for interprocess communications.
7	s
	Socket used for interprocess communication.

Met acharacters

Metacharacters have a special meaning in Unix. For example, *
and ? are metacharacters. We use * to match 0 or more
characters, a question mark (?) matches with a single character.

For Example –

$ls ch*.doc

Displays all the files, the names of which start with ch and end with .doc –

ch01-1.doc ch010.doc ch02.doc   ch03-2.doc
ch04-1.doc ch040.doc ch05.doc   ch06-2.doc
ch01-2.doc ch02-1.doc c

Here, * works as meta character which matches with any character. If you want to display all the files ending with just .doc, then you can use the following command –

$ls *.doc

Hidden Files

An invisible file is one, the first character of which is the dot or the period character (.). Unix programs (including the shell) use most of these files to store configuration information.

Some common examples of the hidden files include the files –

- .profile – The Bourne shell (sh) initialization script
- .kshrc – The Korn shell (ksh) initialization script
- .cshrc – The C shell (csh) initialization script
- .rhosts – The remote shell configuration file

To list the invisible files, specify the -a option to ls –

```
$ ls -a
```

```
.          .profile     docs     lib     test_results
..         .rhosts      hosts    pub     users
.emacs     bin          hw1      res.01  work
.exrc      ch07         hw2      res.02
.kshrc     ch07.bak     hw3      res.03
$
```

- Single dot (.) – This represents the current directory.
- Double dot (..) – This represents the parent directory.

Creating Files

You can use the vi editor to create ordinary files on any Unix system. You simply need to give the following command –

```
$ vi filename
```

The above command will open a file with the given filename. Now, press the key i to come into the edit mode. Once you are in the edit mode, you can start writing your content in the file as in the following program –

```
This is unix file....I created it for the first time.....
I'm going to save this content in this file.
```

Once you are done with the program, follow these steps –

- Press the key esc to come out of the edit mode.
- Press two keys Shift + ZZ together to come out of the file completely.

You will now have a file created with filename in the current directory.

Editing Files

You can edit an existing file using the vi editor. We will discuss in short how to open an existing file −

Once the file is opened, you can come in the edit mode by pressing the key iand then you can proceed by editing the file. If you want to move here and there inside a file, then first you need to come out of the edit mode by pressing the key Esc. After this, you can use the following keys to move inside a file −

- l key to move to the right side.
- h key to move to the left side.
- k key to move upside in the file.
- j key to move downside in the file.

So using the above keys, you can position your cursor wherever you want to edit. Once you are positioned, then you can use the i key to come in the edit mode. Once you are done with the editing in your file, press Esc and finally two keys Shift + ZZ together to come out of the file completely.

Display Content of a File

You can use the cat command to see the content of a file. Following is a simple example to see the content of the above created file –

```
$ cat filename
This is unix file....I created it for the first time.....
I'm going to save this content in this file.
$
```

You can display the line numbers by using the -b option along with the catcommand as follows –

```
$ cat -b filename
1   This is unix file....I created it for the first time.....
2   I'm going to save this content in this file.
$
```

Counting Words in a File

You can use the wc command to get a count of the total number of lines, words, and characters contained in a file. Following is a simple example to see the information about the file created above –

```
$ wc filename
2  19 103 filename
$
```

Here is the detail of all the four columns –

- First Column – Represents the total number of lines in the file.
- Second Column – Represents the total number of words in the file.
- Third Column – Represents the total number of bytes in the file. This is the actual size of the file.
- Fourth Column – Represents the file name.

You can give multiple files and get information about those files at a time. Following is simple syntax –

```
$ wc filename1 filename2 filename3
```

Copying Files

To make a copy of a file use the cp command. The basic syntax of the command is –

```
$ cp source_file destination_file
```

Following is the example to create a copy of the existing file filename.

```
$ cp filename copyfile
$
```

You will now find one more file copyfile in your current directory. This file will exactly be the same as the original file filename.

Renaming Files

To change the name of a file, use the mv command. Following is the basic syntax –

```
$ mv old_file new_file
```

The following program will rename the existing file filename to newfile.

```
$ mv filename newfile
$
```

The mv command will move the existing file completely into the new file. In this case, you will find only newfile in your current directory.

Deleting Files

To delete an existing file, use the rm command. Following is the basic syntax –

```
$ rm filename
```

Caution – A file may contain useful information. It is always recommended to be careful while using this Delete command. It is better to use the -i option along with rm command.

Following is the example which shows how to completely remove the existing file filename.

```
$ rm filename
$
```

You can remove multiple files at a time with the command given below –

```
$ rm filename1 filename2 filename3
$
```

Standard Unix Streams

Under normal circumstances, every Unix program has three streams (files) opened for it when it starts up –

- stdin – This is referred to as the *standard input* and the associated file descriptor is 0. This is also represented as STDIN. The Unix program will read the default input from STDIN.
- stdout – This is referred to as the *standard output* and the associated file descriptor is 1. This is also represented as STDOUT. The Unix program will write the default output at STDOUT
- stderr – This is referred to as the *standard error* and the associated file descriptor is 2. This is also represented as STDERR. The Unix program will write all the error messages at STDERR.

Unix - Directory Management

In this chapter, we will discuss in detail about directory management in Unix.

A directory is a file the solo job of which is to store the file names and the related information. All the files, whether ordinary, special, or directory, are contained in directories.

Unix uses a hierarchical structure for organizing files and directories. This structure is often referred to as a directory tree. The tree has a single root node, the slash character (/), and all other directories are contained below it.

Home Directory

The directory in which you find yourself when you first login is called your home directory.

You will be doing much of your work in your home directory and subdirectories that you'll be creating to organize your files.

You can go in your home directory anytime using the following command –

```
$cd ~
$
```

Here ~ indicates the home directory. Suppose you have to go in any other user's home directory, use the following command –

```
$cd ~username
$
```

To go in your last directory, you can use the following command –

```
$cd -
$
```

Absolute/Relative Pathnames

Directories are arranged in a hierarchy with root (/) at the top. The position of any file within the hierarchy is described by its pathname.

Elements of a pathname are separated by a /. A pathname is absolute, if it is described in relation to root, thus absolute pathnames always begin with a /.

Following are some examples of absolute filenames.

```
/etc/passwd
/users/sjones/chem/notes
/dev/rdsk/Os3
```

A pathname can also be relative to your current working directory. Relative pathnames never begin with /. Relative to user amrood's home directory, some pathnames might look like this –

chem/notes
personal/res

To determine where you are within the filesystem hierarchy at any time, enter the command pwd to print the current working directory –

```
$pwd
/user0/home/amrood

$
```

Listing Directories

To list the files in a directory, you can use the following syntax –

```
$ls dirname
```


Following is the example to list all the files contained in /usr/local directory –

```
$ls /usr/local
```

```
X11     bin     gimp      jikes   sbin
ace     doc     include   lib     share
atalk   etc     info      man     ami
```

Creating Directories

We will now understand how to create directories. Directories are created by the following command –

```
$mkdir dirname
```

Here, directory is the absolute or relative pathname of the directory you want to create. For example, the command –

```
$mkdir mydir
$
```

Creates the directory mydir in the current directory. Here is another example –

```
$mkdir /tmp/test-dir
$
```

This command creates the directory test-dir in the /tmp directory. The mkdir command produces no output if it successfully creates the requested directory.

If you give more than one directory on the command line, mkdir creates each of the directories. For example, –

```
$mkdir docs pub
$
```

Creates the directories docs and pub under the current directory.

Creating Parent Directories

We will now understand how to create parent directories. Sometimes when you want to create a directory, its parent directory or directories might not exist. In this case, mkdir issues an error message as follows —

```
$mkdir /tmp/amrood/test
mkdir: Failed to make directory "/tmp/amrood/test";
No such file or directory
$
```

In such cases, you can specify the -p option to the mkdir command. It creates all the necessary directories for you. For example —

```
$mkdir -p /tmp/amrood/test
$
```

The above command creates all the required parent directories.

Removing Directories

Directories can be deleted using the rmdir command as follows —

```
$rmdir dirname
$
```

Note — To remove a directory, make sure it is empty which means there should not be any file or sub-directory inside this directory.

You can remove multiple directories at a time as follows —

```
$rmdir dirname1 dirname2 dirname3
$
```

The above command removes the directories dirname1, dirname2, and dirname3, if they are empty. The rmdir command produces no output if it is successful.

Changing Directories

You can use the cd command to do more than just change to a home directory. You can use it to change to any directory by specifying a valid absolute or relative path. The syntax is as given below —

```
$cd dirname
$
```

Here, dirname is the name of the directory that you want to change to. For example, the command —

```
$cd /usr/local/bin
$
```

Changes to the directory /usr/local/bin. From this directory, you can cd to the directory /usr/home/amrood using the following relative path —

```
$cd ../../home/amrood
$
```

Renaming Directories

The mv (move) command can also be used to rename a directory. The syntax is as follows —

```
$mv olddir newdir
$
```

You can rename a directory mydir to yourdir as follows −

```
$mv mydir yourdir
$
```

The directories . (dot) and .. (dot dot)

The filename . (dot) represents the current working directory; and the filename .. (dot dot) represents the directory one level above the current working directory, often referred to as the parent directory.

If we enter the command to show a listing of the current working directories/files and use the -a option to list all the files and the -l option to provide the long listing, we will receive the following result.

```
$ls -la
drwxrwxr-x   4   teacher   class   2048  Jul 16 17.56 .
drwxr-xr-x   60  root              1536  Jul 13 14:18 ..
----------   1   teacher   class   4210  May 1 08:27 .profile
-rwxr-xr-x   1   teacher   class   1948  May 12 13:42 memo
$
```

Unix - File Permission / Access Modes

In this chapter, we will discuss in detail about file permission and access modes in Unix. File ownership is an important component of Unix that provides a secure method for storing files. Every file in Unix has the following attributes —

- Owner permissions — The owner's permissions determine what actions the owner of the file can perform on the file.
- Group permissions — The group's permissions determine what actions a user, who is a member of the group that a file belongs to, can perform on the file.
- Other (world) permissions — The permissions for others indicate what action all other users can perform on the file.

The Permission Indicators

While using ls -l command, it displays various information related to file permission as follows —

```
$ls -l /home/amrood
-rwxr-xr--  1 amrood  users 1024  Nov 2 00:10  myfile
drwxr-xr---  1 amrood  users 1024  Nov 2 00:10  mydir
```

Here, the first column represents different access modes, i.e., the permission associated with a file or a directory.

The permissions are broken into groups of threes, and each position in the group denotes a specific permission, in this order: read (r), write (w), execute (x) —

- The first three characters (2-4) represent the permissions for the file's owner. For example, -rwxr-xr-- represents that the owner has read (r), write (w) and execute (x) permission.

- The second group of three characters (5-7) consists of the permissions for the group to which the file belongs. For example, -rwxr-xr--represents that the group has read (r) and execute (x) permission, but no write permission.
- The last group of three characters (8-10) represents the permissions for everyone else. For example, -rwxr-xr-- represents that there is read (r) only permission.

File Access Modes

The permissions of a file are the first line of defense in the security of a Unix system. The basic building blocks of Unix permissions are the read, write, and execute permissions, which have been described below —

Read

Grants the capability to read, i.e., view the contents of the file.

Write

Grants the capability to modify, or remove the content of the file.

Execute

User with execute permissions can run a file as a program.

Directory Access Modes

Directory access modes are listed and organized in the same manner as any other file. There are a few differences that need to be mentioned —

Read

Access to a directory means that the user can read the contents. The user can look at the filenames inside the directory.

Write

Access means that the user can add or delete files from the directory.

Execute

Executing a directory doesn't really make sense, so think of this as a traverse permission.

A user must have execute access to the bin directory in order to execute the ls or the cd command.

Changing Permissions

To change the file or the directory permissions, you use the chmod (change mode) command. There are two ways to use chmod — the symbolic mode and the absolute mode.

Using chmod in Symbolic Mode

The easiest way for a beginner to modify file or directory permissions is to use the symbolic mode. With symbolic permissions you can add, delete, or specify the permission set you want by using the operators in the following table.

S.No.	Chmod operator & Description
1	**+** Adds the designated permission(s) to a file or directory.
2	**-** Removes the designated permission(s) from a file or directory.
3	**=** Sets the designated permission(s).

Here's an example using testfile. Running ls -1 on the testfile shows that the file's permissions are as follows —

```
$ls -l testfile
-rwxrwxr-- 1 amrood   users 1024 Nov 2 00:10 testfile
```

Then each example chmod command from the preceding table is run on the testfile, followed by ls -l, so you can see the permission changes —

```
$chmod o+wx testfile
$ls -l testfile
-rwxrwxrwx 1 amrood   users 1024 Nov 2 00:10 testfile
$chmod u-x testfile
$ls -l testfile
-rw-rwxrwx 1 amrood   users 1024 Nov 2 00:10 testfile
$chmod g = rx testfile
$ls -l testfile
-rw-r-xrwx 1 amrood   users 1024 Nov 2 00:10 testfile
```

Here's how you can combine these commands on a single line —

```
$chmod o+wx,u-x,g = rx testfile
$ls -l testfile
-rw-r-xrwx 1 amrood   users 1024 Nov 2 00:10 testfile
```

Using chmod with Absolute Permissions

The second way to modify permissions with the chmod command is to use a number to specify each set of permissions for the file.

Each permission is assigned a value, as the following table shows, and the total of each set of permissions provides a number for that set.

Number	Octal Permission Representation	Ref
0	No permission	---
1	Execute permission	--x
2	Write permission	-w-
3	Execute and write permission: 1 (execute) + 2 (write) = 3	-wx
4	Read permission	r--
5	Read and execute permission: 4 (read) + 1 (execute) = 5	r-x
6	Read and write permission: 4 (read) + 2 (write) = 6	rw-
7	All permissions: 4 (read) + 2 (write) + 1 (execute) = 7	rwx

Here's an example using the testfile. Running ls -1 on the testfile shows that the file's permissions are as follows —

```
$ls -l testfile
-rwxrwxr-- 1 amrood  users 1024  Nov 2 00:10  testfile
```

Then each example chmod command from the preceding table is run on the testfile, followed by ls –l, so you can see the permission changes —

```
$ chmod 755 testfile
$ls -l testfile
-rwxr-xr-x 1 amrood  users 1024  Nov 2 00:10  testfile
$chmod 743 testfile
$ls -l testfile
-rwxr---wx 1 amrood  users 1024  Nov 2 00:10  testfile
$chmod 043 testfile
$ls -l testfile
----r---wx 1 amrood  users 1024  Nov 2 00:10  testfile
```

Changing Owners and Groups

While creating an account on Unix, it assigns a owner ID and a group ID to each user. All the permissions mentioned above are also assigned based on the Owner and the Groups.

Two commands are available to change the owner and the group of files —

- chown — The chown command stands for "change owner" and is used to change the owner of a file.
- chgrp — The chgrp command stands for "change group" and is used to change the group of a file.

Changing Ownership

The chown command changes the ownership of a file. The basic syntax is as follows —

```
$ chown user filelist
```

The value of the user can be either the name of a user on the system or the user id (uid) of a user on the system.

The following example will help you understand the concept —

```
$ chown amrood testfile
$
```

Changes the owner of the given file to the user amrood.

NOTE — The super user, root, has the unrestricted capability to change the ownership of any file but normal users can change the ownership of only those files that they own.

Changing Group Ownership

The chgrp command changes the group ownership of a file. The basic syntax is as follows —

```
$ chgrp group filelist
```

The value of group can be the name of a group on the system or the group ID (GID) of a group on the system.

Following example helps you understand the concept —

```
$ chgrp special testfile
$
```

Changes the group of the given file to special group.

SUID and SGID File Permission

Often when a command is executed, it will have to be executed with special privileges in order to accomplish its task.

As an example, when you change your password with the passwd command, your new password is stored in the file /etc/shadow.

As a regular user, you do not have read or write access to this file for security reasons, but when you change your password, you need to have the write permission to this file. This means that the passwd program has to give you additional permissions so that you can write to the file /etc/shadow.

Additional permissions are given to programs via a mechanism known as the Set User ID (SUID) and Set Group ID (SGID) bits.

When you execute a program that has the SUID bit enabled, you inherit the permissions of that program's owner. Programs that do not have the SUID bit set are run with the permissions of the user who started the program.

This is the case with SGID as well. Normally, programs execute with your group permissions, but instead your group will be changed just for this program to the group owner of the program.

The SUID and SGID bits will appear as the letter "s" if the permission is available. The SUID "s" bit will be located in the permission bits where the owners' execute permission normally resides.

For example, the command −

```
$ ls -l /usr/bin/passwd
-r-sr-xr-x  1   root  bin  19031 Feb 7 13:47  /usr/bin/passwd*
$
```

Shows that the SUID bit is set and that the command is owned by the root. A capital letter S in the execute position instead of a lowercase s indicates that the execute bit is not set.

If the sticky bit is enabled on the directory, files can only be removed if you are one of the following users −

- The owner of the sticky directory
- The owner of the file being removed
- The super user, root

To set the SUID and SGID bits for any directory try the following command −

```
$ chmod ug+s dirname
$ ls -l
drwsr-sr-x 2 root root  4096 Jun 19 06:45 dirname
```

$

Unix - Environment

In this chapter, we will discuss in detail about the Unix environment. An important Unix concept is the environment, which is defined by environment variables. Some are set by the system, others by you, yet others by the shell, or any program that loads another program.

A variable is a character string to which we assign a value. The value assigned could be a number, text, filename, device, or any other type of data.

For example, first we set a variable TEST and then we access its value using the echo command —

```
$TEST="Unix Programming"
$echo $TEST
```

It produces the following result.

Unix Programming

Note that the environment variables are set without using the $ sign but while accessing them we use the $ sign as prefix. These variables retain their values until we come out of the shell.

When you log in to the system, the shell undergoes a phase called initialization to set up the environment. This is usually a two-step process that involves the shell reading the following files —

- /etc/profile

- profile

The process is as follows −

- The shell checks to see whether the file /etc/profile exists.
- If it exists, the shell reads it. Otherwise, this file is skipped. No error message is displayed.
- The shell checks to see whether the file .profile exists in your home directory. Your home directory is the directory that you start out in after you log in.
- If it exists, the shell reads it; otherwise, the shell skips it. No error message is displayed.

As soon as both of these files have been read, the shell displays a prompt −

$

This is the prompt where you can enter commands in order to have them executed.

Note − The shell initialization process detailed here applies to all Bourne type shells, but some additional files are used by bash and ksh.

The .profile File

The file /etc/profile is maintained by the system administrator of your Unix machine and contains shell initialization information required by all users on a system.

The file .profile is under your control. You can add as much shell customization information as you want to this file. The minimum set of information that you need to configure includes −

- The type of terminal you are using.
- A list of directories in which to locate the commands.

- A list of variables affecting the look and feel of your terminal. You can check your .profile available in your home directory. Open it using the vi editor and check all the variables set for your environment.

Setting the Terminal Type

Usually, the type of terminal you are using is automatically configured by either the login or getty programs. Sometimes, the auto configuration process guesses your terminal incorrectly.

If your terminal is set incorrectly, the output of the commands might look strange, or you might not be able to interact with the shell properly.

To make sure that this is not the case, most users set their terminal to the lowest common denominator in the following way —

```
$TERM=vt100
$
```

Setting the PATH

When you type any command on the command prompt, the shell has to locate the command before it can be executed.

The PATH variable specifies the locations in which the shell should look for commands. Usually the Path variable is set as follows —

```
$PATH = /bin:/usr/bin
$
```

Here, each of the individual entries separated by the colon character (:) are directories. If you request the shell to execute a command and it cannot find it in any of the directories given in the PATH variable, a message similar to the following appears −

```
$hello
hello: not found
$
```

There are variables like PS1 and PS2 which are discussed in the next section.

PS1 and PS2 Variables

The characters that the shell displays as your command prompt are stored in the variable PS1. You can change this variable to be anything you want. As soon as you change it, it'll be used by the shell from that point on.

For example, if you issued the command −

```
$PS1='=>'
=>
=>
=>
```

Your prompt will become =>. To set the value of PS1 so that it shows the working directory, issue the command −

```
=>PS1="[\u@\h \w]\$"
[root@ip-72-167-112-17 /var/www/tutorialspoint/unix]$
[root@ip-72-167-112-17 /var/www/tutorialspoint/unix]$
```

The result of this command is that the prompt displays the user's username, the machine's name (hostname), and the working directory.

There are quite a few escape sequences that can be used as value arguments for PS1; try to limit yourself to the most critical so that the prompt does not overwhelm you with information.

S.No.	Escape Sequence & Description
1	**\t** Current time, expressed as HH:MM:SS
2	**\d** Current date, expressed as Weekday Month Date
3	**\n** Newline
4	**\s** Current shell environment

5	\W	Working directory
6	\w	Full path of the working directory
7	\u	Current user's username
8	\h	Hostname of the current machine
9	\#	Command number of the current command. Increases when a new command is entered

10	\$
	If the effective UID is 0 (that is, if you are logged in as root), end the prompt with the # character; otherwise, use the $ sign

You can make the change yourself every time you log in, or you can have the change made automatically in PS1 by adding it to your .profile file.

When you issue a command that is incomplete, the shell will display a secondary prompt and wait for you to complete the command and hit Enteragain.

The default secondary prompt is > (the greater than sign), but can be changed by re-defining the PS2 shell variable —

Following is the example which uses the default secondary prompt —

```
$ echo "this is a
> test"
this is a
test
$
```

The example given below re-defines PS2 with a customized prompt —

```
$ PS2="secondary prompt->"
$ echo "this is a
secondary prompt->test"
this is a
test
$
```

Environment Variables

Following is the partial list of important environment variables. These variables are set and accessed as mentioned below –

S.No.	Variable & Description
1	**DISPLAY** Contains the identifier for the display that X11 programs should use by default.
2	**HOME** Indicates the home directory of the current user: the default argument for the cd built-in command.
3	**IFS** Indicates the Internal Field Separator that is used by the parser for word splitting after expansion.

4	**LANG**
	LANG expands to the default system locale; LC_ALL can be used to override this. For example, if its value is pt_BR, then the language is set to (Brazilian) Portuguese and the locale to Brazil.
5	**LD_LIBRARY_PATH**
	A Unix system with a dynamic linker, contains a colonseparated list of directories that the dynamic linker should search for shared objects when building a process image after exec, before searching in any other directories.
6	**PATH**
	Indicates the search path for commands. It is a colon-separated list of directories in which the shell looks for commands.
7	**PWD**
	Indicates the current working directory as set by the cd command.

8	**RANDOM**
	Generates a random integer between 0 and 32,767 each time it is referenced.
9	**SHLVL**
	Increments by one each time an instance of bash is started. This variable is useful for determining whether the built-in exit command ends the current session.
10	**TERM**
	Refers to the display type.
11	**TZ**
	Refers to Time zone. It can take values like GMT, AST, etc.
12	**UID**
	Expands to the numeric user ID of the current

user, initialized at the shell startup.

Following is the sample example showing few environment variables —

```
$ echo $HOME
/root
]$ echo $DISPLAY

$ echo $TERM
xterm
$ echo $PATH
/usr/local/bin:/bin:/usr/bin:/home/amrood/bin:/usr/local/bin
$
```

Unix Basic Utilities - Printing, Email

In this chapter, we will discuss in detail about Printing and Email as the basic utilities of Unix. So far, we have tried to understand the Unix OS and the nature of its basic commands. In this chapter, we will learn some important Unix utilities that can be used in our day-to-day life.

Printing Files

Before you print a file on a Unix system, you may want to reformat it to adjust the margins, highlight some words, and so on. Most files can also be printed without reformatting, but the raw printout may not be that appealing.

Many versions of Unix include two powerful text formatters, nroff and troff.

The pr Command

The pr command does minor formatting of files on the terminal screen or for a printer. For example, if you have a long list of names in a file, you can format it onscreen into two or more columns.

Following is the syntax for the pr command –

pr option(s) filename(s)

The pr changes the format of the file only on the screen or on the printed copy; it doesn't modify the original file. Following table lists some pr options —

S.No.	Option & Description
1	**-k** Produces k columns of output
2	**-d** Double-spaces the output (not on all pr versions)
3	**-h "header"** Takes the next item as a report header
4	**-t** Eliminates the printing of header and the top/bottom margins

5	**-I PAGE_LENGTH**
	Sets the page length to PAGE_LENGTH (66) lines. The default number of lines of text is 56
6	**-o MARGIN**
	Offsets each line with MARGIN (zero) spaces
7	**-w PAGE_WIDTH**
	Sets the page width to PAGE_WIDTH (72) characters for multiple text-column output only

Before using pr, here are the contents of a sample file named food.

```
$cat food
Sweet Tooth
Bangkok Wok
Mandalay
Afghani Cuisine
Isle of Java
Big Apple Deli
Sushi and Sashimi
Tio Pepe's Peppers
........
$
```

Let's use the pr command to make a two-column report with the header *Restaurants* —

```
$pr -2 -h "Restaurants" food
Nov  7  9:58 1997  Restaurants   Page 1

Sweet Tooth           Isle of Java
Bangkok Wok           Big Apple Deli
Mandalay              Sushi and Sashimi
Afghani Cuisine       Tio Pepe's Peppers
........
$
```

The lp and lpr Commands

The command lp or lpr prints a file onto paper as opposed to the screen display. Once you are ready with formatting using the pr command, you can use any of these commands to print your file on the printer connected to your computer.

Your system administrator has probably set up a default printer at your site. To print a file named food on the default printer, use the lp or lpr command, as in the following example –

```
$lp food
request id is laserp-525  (1 file)
$
```

The lp command shows an ID that you can use to cancel the print job or check its status.

- If you are using the lp command, you can use the -nNum option to print Num number of copies. Along with the command lpr, you can use -Num for the same.

- If there are multiple printers connected with the shared network, then you can choose a printer using -dprinter option along with lp command and for the same purpose you can use -Pprinter option along with lpr command. Here printer is the printer name.

The lpstat and lpq Commands

The lpstat command shows what's in the printer queue: request IDs, owners, file sizes, when the jobs were sent for printing, and the status of the requests.

Use lpstat -o if you want to see all output requests other than just your own. Requests are shown in the order they'll be printed —

```
$lpstat -o
laserp-573 john  128865 Nov 7  11:27  on laserp
laserp-574 grace 82744 Nov 7  11:28
laserp-575 john   23347 Nov 7  11:35
$
```

The lpq gives slightly different information than lpstat -o —

```
$lpq
laserp is ready and printing
Rank  Owner    Job Files            Total Size
active john     573 report.ps          128865 bytes
1st   grace    574 ch03.ps ch04.ps     82744 bytes
2nd   john     575 standard input      23347 bytes
$
```

Here the first line displays the printer status. If the printer is disabled or running out of paper, you may see different messages on this first line.

The cancel and lprm Commands

The cancel command terminates a printing request from the lp command. The lprm command terminates all lpr requests. You can specify either the ID of the request (displayed by lp or lpq) or the name of the printer.

```
$cancel laserp-575
request "laserp-575" cancelled
$
```

To cancel whatever request is currently printing, regardless of its ID, simply enter cancel and the printer name —

```
$cancel laserp
request "laserp-573" cancelled
$
```

The lprm command will cancel the active job if it belongs to you. Otherwise, you can give job numbers as arguments, or use a dash (-) to remove all of your jobs —

```
$lprm 575
dfA575diamond dequeued
cfA575diamond dequeued
$
```

The lprm command tells you the actual filenames removed from the printer queue.

Sending Email

You use the Unix mail command to send and receive mail. Here is the syntax to send an email —

```
$mail [-s subject] [-c cc-addr] [-b bcc-addr] to-addr
```

Here are important options related to mail command —s

S.No.	Option & Description
1	**-s** Specifies subject on the command line.
2	**-c** Sends carbon copies to the list of users. List should be a commaseparated list of names.
3	**-b** Sends blind carbon copies to list. List should be a commaseparated list of names.

Following is an example to send a test message to admin@yahoo.com.

$mail -s "Test Message" admin@yahoo.com

You are then expected to type in your message, followed by "control-D" at the beginning of a line. To stop, simply type dot (.) as follows —

Hi,

This is a test
.
Cc:

You can send a complete file using a redirect < operator as follows —

```
$mail -s "Report 05/06/07" admin@yahoo.com < demo.txt
```

To check incoming email at your Unix system, you simply type email as follows —

```
$mail
no email
```

Unix - Pipes and Filters

In this chapter, we will discuss in detail about pipes and filters in Unix. You can connect two commands together so that the output from one program becomes the input of the next program. Two or more commands connected in this way form a pipe.

To make a pipe, put a vertical bar (|) on the command line between two commands.

When a program takes its input from another program, it performs some operation on that input, and writes the result to the standard output. It is referred to as a *filter*.

The grep Command

The grep command searches a file or files for lines that have a certain pattern. The syntax is −

$grep pattern file(s)

The name "grep" comes from the ed (a Unix line editor) command g/re/pwhich means "globally search for a regular expression and print all lines containing it".

A regular expression is either some plain text (a word, for example) and/or special characters used for pattern matching.

The simplest use of grep is to look for a pattern consisting of a single word. It can be used in a pipe so that only those lines of the input files containing a given string are sent to the standard output. If you don't give grep a filename to read, it reads its standard input; that's the way all filter programs work —

```
$ls -l | grep "Aug"
-rw-rw-rw-  1 john  doc    11008 Aug  6 14:10 ch02
-rw-rw-rw-  1 john  doc     8515 Aug  6 15:30 ch07
-rw-rw-r--  1 john  doc     2488 Aug 15 10:51 intro
-rw-rw-r--  1 carol doc     1605 Aug 23 07:35 macros
$
```

There are various options which you can use along with the grep command —

S.No.	Option & Description
1	**-v** Prints all lines that do not match pattern.
2	**-n** Prints the matched line and its line number.
3	**-l** Prints only the names of files with matching lines (letter "l")

4	**-c**
	Prints only the count of matching lines.
5	**-i**
	Matches either upper or lowercase.

Let us now use a regular expression that tells grep to find lines with "carol", followed by zero or other characters abbreviated in a regular expression as ".*"), then followed by "Aug".—

Here, we are using the *-i* option to have case insensitive search —

```
$ls -l | grep -i "carol.*aug"
-rw-rw-r--  1 carol doc    1605 Aug 23 07:35 macros
$
```

The sort Command

The sort command arranges lines of text alphabetically or numerically. The following example sorts the lines in the food file —

```
$sort food
Afghani Cuisine
Bangkok Wok
Big Apple Deli
Isle of Java

Mandalay
Sushi and Sashimi
```

Sweet Tooth
Tio Pepe's Peppers
$

The sort command arranges lines of text alphabetically by default. There are many options that control the sorting –

S.No.	Description
1	**-n** Sorts numerically (example: 10 will sort after 2), ignores blanks and tabs.
2	**-r** Reverses the order of sort.
3	**-f** Sorts upper and lowercase together.
4	**+x** Ignores first x fields when sorting.

More than two commands may be linked up into a pipe. Taking a previous pipe example using grep, we can further sort the files modified in August by the order of size.

The following pipe consists of the commands ls, grep, and sort –

```
$ls -l | grep "Aug" | sort +4n
-rw-rw-r--  1 carol doc     1605 Aug 23 07:35 macros
-rw-rw-r--  1 john  doc     2488 Aug 15 10:51 intro
-rw-rw-rw-  1 john  doc     8515 Aug  6 15:30 ch07
-rw-rw-rw-  1 john  doc    11008 Aug  6 14:10 ch02
$
```

This pipe sorts all files in your directory modified in August by the order of size, and prints them on the terminal screen. The sort option +4n skips four fields (fields are separated by blanks) then sorts the lines in numeric order.

The pg and more Commands

A long output can normally be zipped by you on the screen, but if you run text through more or use the pg command as a filter; the display stops once the screen is full of text.

Let's assume that you have a long directory listing. To make it easier to read the sorted listing, pipe the output through more as follows –

```
$ls -l | grep "Aug" | sort +4n | more
-rw-rw-r--  1 carol doc     1605 Aug 23 07:35 macros
-rw-rw-r--  1 john  doc     2488 Aug 15 10:51 intro
-rw-rw-rw-  1 john  doc     8515 Aug  6 15:30 ch07
-rw-rw-r--  1 john  doc    14827 Aug  9 12:40 ch03
      .
      .
      .
-rw-rw-rw-  1 john  doc    16867 Aug  6 15:56 ch05
```

The screen will fill up once the screen is full of text consisting of lines sorted by the order of the file size. At the bottom of the screen is the more prompt, where you can type a command to move through the sorted text.

Once you're done with this screen, you can use any of the commands listed in the discussion of the more program.

Unix - Processes Management

In this chapter, we will discuss in detail about process management in Unix. When you execute a program on your Unix system, the system creates a special environment for that program. This environment contains everything needed for the system to run the program as if no other program were running on the system.

Whenever you issue a command in Unix, it creates, or starts, a new process. When you tried out the ls command to list the directory contents, you started a process. A process, in simple terms, is an instance of a running program.

The operating system tracks processes through a five-digit ID number known as the pid or the process ID. Each process in the system has a unique pid.

Pids eventually repeat because all the possible numbers are used up and the next pid rolls or starts over. At any point of time, no two processes with the same pid exist in the system because it is the pid that Unix uses to track each process.

Starting a Process

When you start a process (run a command), there are two ways you can run it —

- Foreground Processes
- Background Processes

Foreground Processes

By default, every process that you start runs in the foreground. It gets its input from the keyboard and sends its output to the screen.

You can see this happen with the ls command. If you wish to list all the files in your current directory, you can use the following command –

$ls ch*.doc

This would display all the files, the names of which start with ch and end with .doc –

```
ch01-1.doc  ch010.doc ch02.doc   ch03-2.doc
ch04-1.doc  ch040.doc ch05.doc   ch06-2.doc
ch01-2.doc  ch02-1.doc
```

The process runs in the foreground, the output is directed to my screen, and if the ls command wants any input (which it does not), it waits for it from the keyboard.

While a program is running in the foreground and is time-consuming, no other commands can be run (start any other processes) because the prompt would not be available until the program finishes processing and comes out.

Background Processes

A background process runs without being connected to your keyboard. If the background process requires any keyboard input, it waits.

The advantage of running a process in the background is that you can run other commands; you do not have to wait until it completes to start another!

The simplest way to start a background process is to add an ampersand (&) at the end of the command.

$ls ch*.doc &

This displays all those files the names of which start with ch and end with .doc –

ch01-1.doc   ch010.doc ch02.doc   ch03-2.doc
ch04-1.doc   ch040.doc ch05.doc   ch06-2.doc
ch01-2.doc   ch02-1.doc

Here, if the ls command wants any input (which it does not), it goes into a stop state until we move it into the foreground and give it the data from the keyboard.

That first line contains information about the background process - the job number and the process ID. You need to know the job number to manipulate it between the background and the foreground.

Press the Enter key and you will see the following –

[1] + Done   ls ch*.doc &
$

The first line tells you that the ls command background process finishes successfully. The second is a prompt for another command.

Listing Running Processes

It is easy to see your own processes by running the ps (process status) command as follows –

```
$ps
PID     TTY    TIME      CMD
18358   ttyp3  00:00:00  sh
18361   ttyp3  00:01:31  abiword
18789   ttyp3  00:00:00  ps
```

One of the most commonly used flags for ps is the -f (f for full) option, which provides more information as shown in the following example –

```
$ps -f
UID     PID PPID C STIME   TTY  TIME CMD
amrood   6738 3662 0 10:23:03 pts/6 0:00 first_one
amrood   6739 3662 0 10:22:54 pts/6 0:00 second_one
amrood   3662 3657 0 08:10:53 pts/6 0:00 -ksh
amrood   6892 3662 4 10:51:50 pts/6 0:00 ps -f
```

Here is the description of all the fields displayed by ps -f command –

S.No.	Column & Description
1	**UID** User ID that this process belongs to (the person running it)

2	**PID**
	Process ID
3	**PPID**
	Parent process ID (the ID of the process that started it)
4	**C**
	CPU utilization of process
5	**STIME**
	Process start time
6	**TTY**
	Terminal type associated with the process
7	**TIME**
	CPU time taken by the process

S.No.	
8	**CMD**
	The command that started this process

There are other options which can be used along with ps command —

S.No.	Option & Description
1	**-a**
	Shows information about all users
2	**-x**
	Shows information about processes without terminals
3	**-u**
	Shows additional information like -f option
4	**-e**

Displays extended information

Stopping Processes

Ending a process can be done in several different ways. Often, from a console-based command, sending a CTRL + C keystroke (the default interrupt character) will exit the command. This works when the process is running in the foreground mode.

If a process is running in the background, you should get its Job ID using the ps command. After that, you can use the kill command to kill the process as follows −

```
$ps -f
UID     PID  PPID C STIME    TTY  TIME CMD
amrood   6738 3662 0 10:23:03 pts/6 0:00 first_one
amrood   6739 3662 0 10:22:54 pts/6 0:00 second_one
amrood   3662 3657 0 08:10:53 pts/6 0:00 -ksh
amrood   6892 3662 4 10:51:50 pts/6 0:00 ps -f
$kill 6738
Terminated
```

Here, the kill command terminates the first_one process. If a process ignores a regular kill command, you can use kill -9 followed by the process ID as follows −

```
$kill -9 6738
Terminated
```

Parent and Child Processes

Each unix process has two ID numbers assigned to it: The Process ID (pid) and the Parent process ID (ppid). Each user process in the system has a parent process.

Most of the commands that you run have the shell as their parent. Check the ps -f example where this command listed both the process ID and the parent process ID.

Zombie and Orphan Processes

Normally, when a child process is killed, the parent process is updated via a SIGCHLD signal. Then the parent can do some other task or restart a new child as needed. However, sometimes the parent process is killed before its child is killed. In this case, the "parent of all processes," the init process, becomes the new PPID (parent process ID). In some cases, these processes are called orphan processes.

When a process is killed, a ps listing may still show the process with a Z state. This is a zombie or defunct process. The process is dead and not being used. These processes are different from the orphan processes. They have completed execution but still find an entry in the process table.

Daemon Processes

Daemons are system-related background processes that often run with the permissions of root and services requests from other processes.

A daemon has no controlling terminal. It cannot open /dev/tty. If you do a "ps -ef" and look at the tty field, all daemons will have a ? for the tty.

To be precise, a daemon is a process that runs in the background, usually waiting for something to happen that it is capable of working with. For example, a printer daemon waiting for print commands.

If you have a program that calls for lengthy processing, then it's worth to make it a daemon and run it in the background.

The top Command

The top command is a very useful tool for quickly showing processes sorted by various criteria.

It is an interactive diagnostic tool that updates frequently and shows information about physical and virtual memory, CPU usage, load averages, and your busy processes.

Here is the simple syntax to run top command and to see the statistics of CPU utilization by different processes −

$top

Job ID Versus Process ID

Background and suspended processes are usually manipulated via job number (job ID). This number is different from the process ID and is used because it is shorter.

In addition, a job can consist of multiple processes running in a series or at the same time, in parallel. Using the job ID is easier than tracking individual processes.

Unix - Network Communication Utilities

In this chapter, we will discuss in detail about network communication utilities in Unix. When you work in a distributed environment, you need to communicate with remote users and you also need to access remote Unix machines.

There are several Unix utilities that help users compute in a networked, distributed environment. This chapter lists a few of them.

The ping Utility

The ping command sends an echo request to a host available on the network. Using this command, you can check if your remote host is responding well or not.

The ping command is useful for the following —

- Tracking and isolating hardware and software problems.
- Determining the status of the network and various foreign hosts.
- Testing, measuring, and managing networks.

Syntax

Following is the simple syntax to use the ping command —

$ping hostname or ip-address

The above command starts printing a response after every second. To come out of the command, you can terminate it by pressing CNTRL + C keys.

Example

Following is an example to check the availability of a host available on the network −

```
$ping google.com
PING google.com (74.125.67.100) 56(84) bytes of data.
64 bytes from 74.125.67.100: icmp_seq = 1 ttl = 54 time = 39.4 ms
64 bytes from 74.125.67.100: icmp_seq = 2 ttl = 54 time = 39.9 ms
64 bytes from 74.125.67.100: icmp_seq = 3 ttl = 54 time = 39.3 ms
64 bytes from 74.125.67.100: icmp_seq = 4 ttl = 54 time = 39.1 ms
64 bytes from 74.125.67.100: icmp_seq = 5 ttl = 54 time = 38.8 ms
--- google.com ping statistics ---
22 packets transmitted, 22 received, 0% packet loss, time 21017ms
rtt min/avg/max/mdev = 38.867/39.334/39.900/0.396 ms
$
```

If a host does not exist, you will receive the following output −

```
$ping giiiiigle.com
ping: unknown host giiiiigle.com
$
```

The ftp Utility

Here, ftp stands for File Transfer Protocol. This utility helps you upload and download your file from one computer to another computer.

The ftp utility has its own set of Unix-like commands. These commands help you perform tasks such as −

- Connect and login to a remote host.

- Navigate directories.
- List directory contents.
- Put and get files.
- Transfer files as ascii, ebcdic or binary.

Syntax

Following is the simple syntax to use the ping command –

$ftp hostname or ip-address

The above command would prompt you for the login ID and the password. Once you are authenticated, you can access the home directory of the login account and you would be able to perform various commands.

The following tables lists out a few important commands –

S.No.	Command & Description
1	**put filename** Uploads filename from the local machine to the remote machine.
2	**get filename** Downloads filename from the remote machine to the local machine.

3	**mput file list** Uploads more than one file from the local machine to the remote machine.
4	**mget file list** Downloads more than one file from the remote machine to the local machine.
5	**prompt off** Turns the prompt off. By default, you will receive a prompt to upload or download files using mput or mget commands.
6	**prompt on** Turns the prompt on.
7	**dir** Lists all the files available in the current directory of the remote machine.

8	**cd dirname**
	Changes directory to dirname on the remote machine.
9	**lcd dirname**
	Changes directory to dirname on the local machine.
10	**quit**
	Helps logout from the current login.

It should be noted that all the files would be downloaded or uploaded to or from the current directories. If you want to upload your files in a particular directory, you need to first change to that directory and then upload the required files.

Example

Following is the example to show the working of a few commands —

```
$ftp amrood.com
Connected to amrood.com.
220 amrood.com FTP server (Ver 4.9 Thu Sep 2 20:35:07 CDT 2009)
Name (amrood.com:amrood): amrood
331 Password required for amrood.
Password:
```

```
230 User amrood logged in.
ftp> dir
200 PORT command successful.
150 Opening data connection for /bin/ls.
total 1464
drwxr-sr-x   3 amrood   group      1024 Mar 11 20:04 Mail
drwxr-sr-x   2 amrood   group      1536 Mar  3 18:07 Misc
drwxr-sr-x   5 amrood   group       512 Dec  7 10:59 OldStuff
drwxr-sr-x   2 amrood   group      1024 Mar 11 15:24 bin
drwxr-sr-x   5 amrood   group      3072 Mar 13 16:10 mpl
-rw-r--r--   1 amrood   group    209671 Mar 15 10:57 myfile.out
drwxr-sr-x   3 amrood   group       512 Jan  5 13:32 public
drwxr-sr-x   3 amrood   group       512 Feb 10 10:17 pvm3
226 Transfer complete.
ftp> cd mpl
250 CWD command successful.
ftp> dir
200 PORT command successful.
150 Opening data connection for /bin/ls.
total 7320
-rw-r--r--   1 amrood   group      1630 Aug  8 1994  dboard.f
-rw-r-----   1 amrood   group      4340 Jul 17 1994  vttest.c
-rwxr-xr-x   1 amrood   group    525574 Feb 15 11:52 wave_shift
-rw-r--r--   1 amrood   group      1648 Aug  5 1994  wide.list
-rwxr-xr-x   1 amrood   group      4019 Feb 14 16:26 fix.c
226 Transfer complete.
ftp> get wave_shift
200 PORT command successful.
150 Opening data connection for wave_shift (525574 bytes).
226 Transfer complete.
528454 bytes received in 1.296 seconds (398.1 Kbytes/s)
ftp> quit
221 Goodbye.
$
```

The telnet Utility

There are times when we are required to connect to a remote Unix machine and work on that machine remotely. Telnet is a utility that allows a computer user at one site to make a connection, login and then conduct work on a computer at another site.

Once you login using Telnet, you can perform all the activities on your remotely connected machine. The following is an example of Telnet session —

```
C:>telnet amrood.com
Trying...
Connected to amrood.com.
Escape character is '^]'.

login: amrood
amrood's Password:
*********************************************************
*                                                       *
*                                                       *
*   WELCOME TO AMROOD.COM                       *
*                                                       *
*                                                       *
*********************************************************

Last unsuccessful login: Fri Mar  3 12:01:09 IST 2009
Last login: Wed Mar  8 18:33:27 IST 2009 on pts/10

   { do your work }

$ logout
Connection closed.
C:>
```

The finger Utility

The finger command displays information about users on a given host. The host can be either local or remote.

Finger may be disabled on other systems for security reasons.

Following is the simple syntax to use the finger command —Check all the logged-in users on the local machine —

```
$ finger
Login    Name    Tty    Idle Login Time   Office
amrood           pts/0        Jun 25 08:03 (62.61.164.115)
```

Get information about a specific user available on the local machine —

```
$ finger amrood
Login: amrood              Name: (null)
Directory: /home/amrood        Shell: /bin/bash
On since Thu Jun 25 08:03 (MST) on pts/0 from 62.61.164.115
No mail.
No Plan.
```

Check all the logged-in users on the remote machine —

```
$ finger @avtar.com
Login    Name    Tty    Idle Login Time   Office
amrood           pts/0        Jun 25 08:03 (62.61.164.115)
```

Get the information about a specific user available on the remote machine —

```
$ finger amrood@avtar.com
Login: amrood              Name: (null)
Directory: /home/amrood        Shell: /bin/bash
On since Thu Jun 25 08:03 (MST) on pts/0 from 62.61.164.115
No mail.
No Plan.
```

Unix - The vi Editor Tutorial

In this chapter, we will understand how the vi Editor works in Unix. There are many ways to edit files in Unix. Editing files using the screen-oriented text editor vi is one of the best ways. This editor enables you to edit lines in context with other lines in the file.

An improved version of the vi editor which is called the VIM has also been made available now. Here, VIM stands for Vi IMproved.

vi is generally considered the de facto standard in Unix editors because −

- It's usually available on all the flavors of Unix system.
- Its implementations are very similar across the board.
- It requires very few resources.
- It is more user-friendly than other editors such as the ed or the ex.

You can use the vi editor to edit an existing file or to create a new file from scratch. You can also use this editor to just read a text file.

Starting the vi Editor

The following table lists out the basic commands to use the vi editor −

S.No.	Command & Description
1	**vi filename** Creates a new file if it already does not exist, otherwise opens an existing file.
2	**vi -R filename** Opens an existing file in the read-only mode.
3	**view filename** Opens an existing file in the read-only mode.

Following is an example to create a new file testfile if it already does not exist in the current working directory −

$vi testfile

The above command will generate the following output —

```
|
~
~
~
~
~
~
~
~
~
~
~
~
~
"testfile" [New File]
```

You will notice a tilde (~) on each line following the cursor. A tilde represents an unused line. If a line does not begin with a tilde and appears to be blank, there is a space, tab, newline, or some other non-viewable character present.

You now have one open file to start working on. Before proceeding further, let us understand a few important concepts.

Operation Modes

While working with the vi editor, we usually come across the following two modes —

- Command mode — This mode enables you to perform administrative tasks such as saving the files, executing the commands, moving the cursor, cutting (yanking) and pasting the lines or words, as well as finding and replacing. In this mode, whatever you type is interpreted as a command.

- Insert mode — This mode enables you to insert text into the file. Everything that's typed in this mode is interpreted as input and placed in the file.

vi always starts in the command mode. To enter text, you must be in the insert mode for which simply type i. To come out of the insert mode, press the Esc key, which will take you back to the command mode.

Hint — If you are not sure which mode you are in, press the Esc key twice; this will take you to the command mode. You open a file using the vi editor. Start by typing some characters and then come to the command mode to understand the difference.

Getting Out of vi

The command to quit out of vi is :q. Once in the command mode, type colon, and 'q', followed by return. If your file has been modified in any way, the editor will warn you of this, and not let you quit. To ignore this message, the command to quit out of vi without saving is :q!. This lets you exit vi without saving any of the changes.

The command to save the contents of the editor is :w. You can combine the above command with the quit command, or use :wq and return.

The easiest way to save your changes and exit vi is with the ZZ command. When you are in the command mode, type ZZ. The ZZ command works the same way as the :wq command.

If you want to specify/state any particular name for the file, you can do so by specifying it after the :w. For example, if you wanted to save the file you were working on as another filename called filename2, you would type :w filename2 and return.

Moving within a File

To move around within a file without affecting your text, you must be in the command mode (press Esc twice). The following table lists out a few commands you can use to move around one character at a time —

S.No.	Command & Description
1	**k** Moves the cursor up one line
2	**j** Moves the cursor down one line
3	**h** Moves the cursor to the left one character position
4	**l** Moves the cursor to the right one character position

The following points need to be considered to move within a file —

- vi is case-sensitive. You need to pay attention to capitalization when using the commands.
- Most commands in vi can be prefaced by the number of times you want the action to occur. For example, 2j moves the cursor two lines down the cursor location.

There are many other ways to move within a file in vi. Remember that you must be in the command mode (press Esc twice). The following table lists out a few commands to move around the file —

Given below is the list of commands to move around the file.

Control Commands

The following commands can be used with the Control Key to performs functions as given in the table below —

Given below is the list of control commands.

Editing Files

To edit the file, you need to be in the insert mode. There are many ways to enter the insert mode from the command mode —

S.No.	Command & Description
1	i

		Inserts text before the current cursor location
2	**I**	Inserts text at the beginning of the current line
3	**a**	Inserts text after the current cursor location
4	**A**	Inserts text at the end of the current line
5	**o**	Creates a new line for text entry below the cursor location
6	**O**	Creates a new line for text entry above the cursor location

Deleting Characters

Here is a list of important commands, which can be used to delete characters and lines in an open file –

S.No.	Command & Description
1	**x** Deletes the character under the cursor location
2	**X** Deletes the character before the cursor location
3	**dw** Deletes from the current cursor location to the next word
4	**d^** Deletes from the current cursor position to the beginning of the line

5	**d$**
	Deletes from the current cursor position to the end of the line
6	**D**
	Deletes from the cursor position to the end of the current line
7	**dd**
	Deletes the line the cursor is on

As mentioned above, most commands in vi can be prefaced by the number of times you want the action to occur. For example, 2x deletes two characters under the cursor location and 2dd deletes two lines the cursor is on.

It is recommended that the commands are practiced before we proceed further.

Change Commands

You also have the capability to change characters, words, or lines in vi without deleting them. Here are the relevant commands —

S.No.	Command & Description
1	**cc** Removes the contents of the line, leaving you in insert mode.
2	**cw** Changes the word the cursor is on from the cursor to the lowercase w end of the word.
3	**r** Replaces the character under the cursor. vi returns to the command mode after the replacement is entered.

4	**R**
	Overwrites multiple characters beginning with the character currently under the cursor. You must use Esc to stop the overwriting.
5	**s**
	Replaces the current character with the character you type. Afterward, you are left in the insert mode.
6	**S**
	Deletes the line the cursor is on and replaces it with the new text. After the new text is entered, vi remains in the insert mode.

Copy and Paste Commands

You can copy lines or words from one place and then you can paste them at another place using the following commands –

S.No.	Command & Description
1	**yy** Copies the current line.
2	**yw** Copies the current word from the character the lowercase w cursor is on, until the end of the word.
3	**p** Puts the copied text after the cursor.
4	**P** Puts the yanked text before the cursor.

Advanced Commands

There are some advanced commands that simplify day-to-day editing and allow for more efficient use of vi —

Given below is the list advanced commands.

Word and Character Searching

The vi editor has two kinds of searches: string and character. For a string search, the / and ? commands are used. When you start these commands, the command just typed will be shown on the last line of the screen, where you type the particular string to look for.

These two commands differ only in the direction where the search takes place —

- The / command searches forwards (downwards) in the file.
- The ? command searches backwards (upwards) in the file.

The n and N commands repeat the previous search command in the same or the opposite direction, respectively. Some characters have special meanings. These characters must be preceded by a backslash (\) to be included as part of the search expression.

S.No.	Character &Description
1	^ Searches at the beginning of the line (Use at the beginning of a search expression).
2	. Matches a single character.
3	* Matches zero or more of the previous character.
4	$ End of the line (Use at the end of the search expression).

5	[
	Starts a set of matching or non-matching expressions.
6	<
	This is put in an expression escaped with the backslash to find the ending or the beginning of a word.
7	>
	This helps see the '<' character description above.

The character search searches within one line to find a character entered after the command. The f and F commands search for a character on the current line only. f searches forwards and F searches backwards and the cursor moves to the position of the found character.

The t and T commands search for a character on the current line only, but for t, the cursor moves to the position before the character, and T searches the line backwards to the position after the character.

Set Commands

You can change the look and feel of your vi screen using the following :setcommands. Once you are in the command mode, type :set followed by any of the following commands.

S.No.	Command & Description
1	**:set ic** Ignores the case when searching
2	**:set ai** Sets autoindent
3	**:set noai** Unsets autoindent
4	**:set nu** Displays lines with line numbers on the left side

5	**:set sw**
	Sets the width of a software tabstop. For example, you would set a shift width of 4 with this command — :set sw = 4
6	**:set ws**
	If *wrapscan* is set, and the word is not found at the bottom of the file, it will try searching for it at the beginning
7	**:set wm**
	If this option has a value greater than zero, the editor will automatically "word wrap". For example, to set the wrap margin to two characters, you would type this: :set wm = 2
8	**:set ro**
	Changes file type to "read only"

9	**:set term** Prints terminal type
10	**:set bf** Discards control characters from input

Running Commands

The vi has the capability to run commands from within the editor. To run a command, you only need to go to the command mode and type :! command.

For example, if you want to check whether a file exists before you try to save your file with that filename, you can type :! ls and you will see the output of ls on the screen.

You can press any key (or the command's escape sequence) to return to your vi session.

Replacing Text

The substitution command (:s/) enables you to quickly replace words or groups of words within your files. Following is the syntax to replace text —

:s/search/replace/g

The g stands for globally. The result of this command is that all occurrences on the cursor's line are changed.

Important Points to Note

The following points will add to your success with vi —

- You must be in command mode to use the commands. (Press Esc twice at any time to ensure that you are in command mode.)
- You must be careful with the commands. These are case-sensitive.
- You must be in insert mode to enter text.

Unix - What is Shells?

A Shell provides you with an interface to the Unix system. It gathers input from you and executes programs based on that input. When a program finishes executing, it displays that program's output.

Shell is an environment in which we can run our commands, programs, and shell scripts. There are different flavors of a shell, just as there are different flavors of operating systems. Each flavor of shell has its own set of recognized commands and functions.

Shell Prompt

The prompt, $, which is called the command prompt, is issued by the shell. While the prompt is displayed, you can type a command.

Shell reads your input after you press Enter. It determines the command you want executed by looking at the first word of your input. A word is an unbroken set of characters. Spaces and tabs separate words.

Following is a simple example of the date command, which displays the current date and time —

```
$date
Thu Jun 25 08:30:19 MST 2009
```

You can customize your command prompt using the environment variable PS1 explained in the Environment tutorial.

Shell Types

In Unix, there are two major types of shells —

- Bourne shell — If you are using a Bourne-type shell, the $ character is the default prompt.
- C shell — If you are using a C-type shell, the % character is the default prompt.

The Bourne Shell has the following subcategories —

- Bourne shell (sh)
- Korn shell (ksh)
- Bourne Again shell (bash)
- POSIX shell (sh)

The different C-type shells follow —

- C shell (csh)
- TENEX/TOPS C shell (tcsh)

The original Unix shell was written in the mid-1970s by Stephen R. Bourne while he was at the AT&T Bell Labs in New Jersey.

Bourne shell was the first shell to appear on Unix systems, thus it is referred to as "the shell".

Bourne shell is usually installed as /bin/sh on most versions of Unix. For this reason, it is the shell of choice for writing scripts that can be used on different versions of Unix.

In this chapter, we are going to cover most of the Shell concepts that are based on the Borne Shell.

Shell Scripts

The basic concept of a shell script is a list of commands, which are listed in the order of execution. A good shell script will have comments, preceded by #sign, describing the steps.

There are conditional tests, such as value A is greater than value B, loops allowing us to go through massive amounts of data, files to read and store data, and variables to read and store data, and the script may include functions.

We are going to write many scripts in the next sections. It would be a simple text file in which we would put all our commands and several other required constructs that tell the shell environment what to do and when to do it.

Shell scripts and functions are both interpreted. This means they are not compiled.

Example Script

Assume we create a test.sh script. Note all the scripts would have the .shextension. Before you add anything else to your script, you need to alert the system that a shell script is being started. This is done using the shebangconstruct. For example —

```
#!/bin/sh
```

This tells the system that the commands that follow are to be executed by the Bourne shell. *It's called a shebang because the # symbol is called a hash, and the ! symbol is called a bang.*

To create a script containing these commands, you put the shebang line first and then add the commands —

```
#!/bin/bash
pwd
ls
```

Shell Comments

You can put your comments in your script as follows —

```
#!/bin/bash

# Author : Zara Ali
# Copyright (c) Tutorialspoint.com
# Script follows here:
pwd
ls
```

Save the above content and make the script executable —

```
$chmod +x test.sh
```

The shell script is now ready to be executed —

```
$./test.sh
```

Upon execution, you will receive the following result —

```
/home/amrood
index.htm  unix-basic_utilities.htm  unix-directories.htm
test.sh  unix-communication.htm  unix-environment.htm
```

Note — To execute a program available in the current directory, use ./program_name

Extended Shell Scripts

Shell scripts have several required constructs that tell the shell environment what to do and when to do it. Of course, most scripts are more complex than the above one.

The shell is, after all, a real programming language, complete with variables, control structures, and so forth. No matter how complicated a script gets, it is still just a list of commands executed sequentially.

The following script uses the read command which takes the input from the keyboard and assigns it as the value of the variable PERSON and finally prints it on STDOUT.

```
#!/bin/sh

# Author : Zara Ali
# Copyright (c) Tutorialspoint.com
# Script follows here:

echo "What is your name?"
read PERSON
echo "Hello, $PERSON"
```

Here is a sample run of the script —

```
$./test.sh
What is your name?
Zara Ali
Hello, Zara Ali
$
```

Unix - Using Shell Variables

In this chapter, we will learn how to use Shell variables in Unix. A variable is a character string to which we assign a value. The value assigned could be a number, text, filename, device, or any other type of data.

A variable is nothing more than a pointer to the actual data. The shell enables you to create, assign, and delete variables.

Variable Names

The name of a variable can contain only letters (a to z or A to Z), numbers (0 to 9) or the underscore character (_).

By convention, Unix shell variables will have their names in UPPERCASE.

The following examples are valid variable names —

```
_ALI
TOKEN_A
VAR_1
VAR_2
```

Following are the examples of invalid variable names —

```
2_VAR
-VARIABLE
VAR1-VAR2
VAR_A!
```

The reason you cannot use other characters such as !, *, or - is that these characters have a special meaning for the shell.

Defining Variables

Variables are defined as follows —

variable_name=variable_value

For example —

NAME="Zara Ali"

The above example defines the variable NAME and assigns the value "Zara Ali" to it. Variables of this type are called scalar variables. A scalar variable can hold only one value at a time.

Shell enables you to store any value you want in a variable. For example —

```
VAR1="Zara Ali"
VAR2=100
```

Accessing Values

To access the value stored in a variable, prefix its name with the dollar sign ($) —

For example, the following script will access the value of defined variable NAME and print it on STDOUT —

```
#!/bin/sh
```

```
NAME="Zara Ali"
echo $NAME
```

The above script will produce the following value —

Zara Ali

Read-only Variables

Shell provides a way to mark variables as read-only by using the read-only command. After a variable is marked read-only, its value cannot be changed.

For example, the following script generates an error while trying to change the value of NAME —

```
#!/bin/sh

NAME="Zara Ali"
readonly NAME
NAME="Qadiri"
```

The above script will generate the following result —

```
/bin/sh: NAME: This variable is read only.
```

Unsetting Variables

Unsetting or deleting a variable directs the shell to remove the variable from the list of variables that it tracks. Once you unset a variable, you cannot access the stored value in the variable.

Following is the syntax to unset a defined variable using the unset command —

```
unset variable_name
```

The above command unsets the value of a defined variable. Here is a simple example that demonstrates how the command works —

```
#!/bin/sh
```

```
NAME="Zara Ali"
unset NAME
echo $NAME
```

The above example does not print anything. You cannot use the unset command to unset variables that are marked readonly.

Variable Types

When a shell is running, three main types of variables are present —

- Local Variables — A local variable is a variable that is present within the current instance of the shell. It is not available to programs that are started by the shell. They are set at the command prompt.
- Environment Variables — An environment variable is available to any child process of the shell. Some programs need environment variables in order to function correctly. Usually, a shell script defines only those environment variables that are needed by the programs that it runs.
- Shell Variables — A shell variable is a special variable that is set by the shell and is required by the shell in order to function correctly. Some of these variables are environment variables whereas others are local variables.

Unix - Special Variables

In this chapter, we will discuss in detail about special variable in Unix. In one of our previous chapters, we understood how to be careful when we use certain nonalphanumeric characters in variable names. This is because those characters are used in the names of special Unix variables. These variables are reserved for specific functions.

For example, the $ character represents the process ID number, or PID, of the current shell —

$echo $$

The above command writes the PID of the current shell —

29949

The following table shows a number of special variables that you can use in your shell scripts —

S.No.	Variable & Description
1	**$0** The filename of the current script.

2	**$n** These variables correspond to the arguments with which a script was invoked. Here n is a positive decimal number corresponding to the position of an argument (the first argument is $1, the second argument is $2, and so on).
3	**$#** The number of arguments supplied to a script.
4	**$*** All the arguments are double quoted. If a script receives two arguments, $* is equivalent to $1 $2.
5	**$@** All the arguments are individually double quoted. If a script receives two arguments, $@ is equivalent to $1 $2.

6	**$?**
	The exit status of the last command executed.
7	**$$**
	The process number of the current shell. For shell scripts, this is the process ID under which they are executing.
8	**$!**
	The process number of the last background command.

Command-Line Arguments

The command-line arguments $1, $2, $3, ...$9 are positional parameters, with $0 pointing to the actual command, program, shell script, or function and $1, $2, $3, ...$9 as the arguments to the command.

Following script uses various special variables related to the command line —

```
#!/bin/sh

echo "File Name: $0"
echo "First Parameter : $1"
echo "Second Parameter : $2"
echo "Quoted Values: $@"
echo "Quoted Values: $*"
echo "Total Number of Parameters : $#"
```

Here is a sample run for the above script —

```
$./test.sh Zara Ali
File Name : ./test.sh
First Parameter : Zara
Second Parameter : Ali
Quoted Values: Zara Ali
Quoted Values: Zara Ali
Total Number of Parameters : 2
```

Special Parameters $* and $@

There are special parameters that allow accessing all the command-line arguments at once. $* and $@ both will act the same unless they are enclosed in double quotes, "".

Both the parameters specify the command-line arguments. However, the "$*" special parameter takes the entire list as one argument with spaces between and the "$@" special parameter takes the entire list and separates it into separate arguments.

We can write the shell script as shown below to process an unknown number of commandline arguments with either the $* or $@ special parameters —

```
#!/bin/sh

for TOKEN in $*
do
   echo $TOKEN
done
```

Here is a sample run for the above script —

```
$./test.sh Zara Ali 10 Years Old
Zara
Ali
10
Years
Old
```

Note — Here do...done is a kind of loop that will be covered in a subsequent tutorial.

Exit Status

The $? variable represents the exit status of the previous command.

Exit status is a numerical value returned by every command upon its completion. As a rule, most commands return an exit status of 0 if they were successful, and 1 if they were unsuccessful.

Some commands return additional exit statuses for particular reasons. For example, some commands differentiate between kinds of errors and will return various exit values depending on the specific type of failure.

Following is the example of successful command —

```
$./test.sh Zara Ali
File Name : ./test.sh
First Parameter : Zara
Second Parameter : Ali
Quoted Values: Zara Ali
Quoted Values: Zara Ali
Total Number of Parameters : 2
$echo $?
0
$
```

Unix - Using Shell Arrays

In this chapter, we will discuss how to use shell arrays in Unix. A shell variable is capable enough to hold a single value. These variables are called scalar variables.

Shell supports a different type of variable called an array variable. This can hold multiple values at the same time. Arrays provide a method of grouping a set of variables. Instead of creating a new name for each variable that is required, you can use a single array variable that stores all the other variables.

All the naming rules discussed for Shell Variables would be applicable while naming arrays.

Defining Array Values

The difference between an array variable and a scalar variable can be explained as follows.

Suppose you are trying to represent the names of various students as a set of variables. Each of the individual variables is a scalar variable as follows —

```
NAME01="Zara"
NAME02="Qadir"
NAME03="Mahnaz"
NAME04="Ayan"
NAME05="Daisy"
```

We can use a single array to store all the above mentioned names. Following is the simplest method of creating an array variable. This helps assign a value to one of its indices.

```
array_name[index]=value
```

Here *array_name* is the name of the array, *index* is the index of the item in the array that you want to set, and value is the value you want to set for that item.

As an example, the following commands –

```
NAME[0]="Zara"
NAME[1]="Qadir"
NAME[2]="Mahnaz"
NAME[3]="Ayan"
NAME[4]="Daisy"
```

If you are using the ksh shell, here is the syntax of array initialization –

```
set -A array_name value1 value2 ... valuen
```

If you are using the bash shell, here is the syntax of array initialization –

```
array_name = (value1 ... valuen)
```

Accessing Array Values

After you have set any array variable, you access it as follows –

```
${array_name[index]}
```

Here *array_name* is the name of the array, and *index* is the index of the value to be accessed. Following is an example to understand the concept –

```
#!/bin/sh

NAME[0]="Zara"
NAME[1]="Qadir"
NAME[2]="Mahnaz"
NAME[3]="Ayan"
NAME[4]="Daisy"
echo "First Index: ${NAME[0]}"
echo "Second Index: ${NAME[1]}"
```

The above example will generate the following result −

```
$./test.sh
First Index: Zara
Second Index: Qadir
```

You can access all the items in an array in one of the following ways −

```
${array_name[*]}
${array_name[@]}
```

Here array_name is the name of the array you are interested in. Following example will help you understand the concept —

```
#!/bin/sh

NAME[0]="Zara"
NAME[1]="Qadir"
NAME[2]="Mahnaz"
NAME[3]="Ayan"
NAME[4]="Daisy"
echo "First Method: ${NAME[*]}"
echo "Second Method: ${NAME[@]}"
```

The above example will generate the following result —

```
$./test.sh
First Method: Zara Qadir Mahnaz Ayan Daisy
Second Method: Zara Qadir Mahnaz Ayan Daisy
```

Unix - Shell Basic Operators

There are various operators supported by each shell. We will discuss in detail about Bourne shell (default shell) in this chapter.

We will now discuss the following operators −

- Arithmetic Operators
- Relational Operators
- Boolean Operators
- String Operators
- File Test Operators

Bourne shell didn't originally have any mechanism to perform simple arithmetic operations but it uses external programs, either awk or expr.

The following example shows how to add two numbers −

```
#!/bin/sh
```

```
val=`expr 2 + 2`
echo "Total value : $val"
```

The above script will generate the following result −

```
Total value : 4
```

The following points need to be considered while adding −

- There must be spaces between operators and expressions. For example, 2+2 is not correct; it should be written as 2 + 2.
- The complete expression should be enclosed between ` `, called the backtick.

Arithmetic Operators

The following arithmetic operators are supported by Bourne Shell.

Assume variable a holds 10 and variable b holds 20 then –

Operator	Description	Example
+ (Addition)	Adds values on either side of the operator	`expr $a + $b` will give 30
- (Subtraction)	Subtracts right hand operand from left hand operand	`expr $a - $b` will give -10
* (Multiplicatio n)	Multiplies values on either side of the operator	`expr $a \* $b` will give 200
/ (Division)	Divides left hand operand by right hand operand	`expr $b / $a` will give 2
% (Modulus)	Divides left hand operand by right hand operand and returns remainder	`expr $b % $a` will give 0

= (Assignment)	Assigns right operand in left operand	a = $b would assign value of b into a
== (Equality)	Compares two numbers, if both are same then returns true.	[$a == $b] would return false.
!= (Not Equality)	Compares two numbers, if both are different then returns true.	[$a != $b] would return true.

It is very important to understand that all the conditional expressions should be inside square braces with spaces around them, for example [$a == $b]is correct whereas, [$a==$b] is incorrect.

All the arithmetical calculations are done using long integers.

Relational Operators

Bourne Shell supports the following relational operators that are specific to numeric values. These operators do not work for string values unless their value is numeric.

For example, following operators will work to check a relation between 10 and 20 as well as in between "10" and "20" but not in between "ten" and "twenty".

Assume variable a holds 10 and variable b holds 20 then —

Opera tor	Description	Example
-eq	Checks if the value of two operands are equal or not; if yes, then the condition becomes true.	[$a -eq $b] is not true.
-ne	Checks if the value of two operands are equal or not; if values are not equal, then the condition becomes true.	[$a -ne $b] is true.
-gt	Checks if the value of left operand is greater than the value of right operand; if yes, then the condition becomes true.	[$a -gt $b] is not true.
-lt	Checks if the value of left operand is less than the value of right operand; if yes, then the condition becomes true.	[$a -lt $b] is true.
-ge	Checks if the value of left operand is greater than or equal to the value of right operand; if yes, then	[$a -ge $b] is not true.

	the condition becomes true.	
-le	Checks if the value of left operand is less than or equal to the value of right operand; if yes, then the condition becomes true.	[$a -le $b] is true.

It is very important to understand that all the conditional expressions should be placed inside square braces with spaces around them. For example, [$a <= $b] is correct whereas, [$a <= $b] is incorrect.

Boolean Operators

The following Boolean operators are supported by the Bourne Shell.

Assume variable a holds 10 and variable b holds 20 then −

Operator	Description	Example
!	This is logical negation. This inverts a true condition into false and vice versa.	[! false] is true.
-o	This is logical **OR**. If one of the operands is true, then the condition becomes true.	[$a -lt 20 -o $b -gt 100] is true.
-a	This is logical **AND**. If both the operands are true, then the condition becomes true otherwise false.	[$a -lt 20 -a $b -gt 100] is false.

String Operators

The following string operators are supported by Bourne Shell.

Assume variable a holds "abc" and variable b holds "efg" then —

Opera tor	Description	Example
=	Checks if the value of two operands are equal or not; if yes, then the condition becomes true.	[$a = $b] is not true.
!=	Checks if the value of two operands are equal or not; if values are not equal then the condition becomes true.	[$a != $b] is true.
-z	Checks if the given string operand size is zero; if it is zero length, then it returns true.	[-z $a] is not true.
-n	Checks if the given string operand size is non-zero; if it is nonzero length, then it returns true.	[-n $a] is not false.
str	Checks if **str** is not the empty string; if it is empty, then it returns false.	[$a] is not false.

File Test Operators

We have a few operators that can be used to test various properties associated with a Unix file.

Assume a variable file holds an existing file name "test" the size of which is 100 bytes and has read, write and execute permission on —

Opera tor	Description	Example
-b file	Checks if file is a block special file; if yes, then the condition becomes true.	[-b $file] is false.
-c file	Checks if file is a character special file; if yes, then the condition becomes true.	[-c $file] is false.
-d file	Checks if file is a directory; if yes, then the condition becomes true.	[-d $file] is not true.
-f file	Checks if file is an ordinary file as opposed to a directory or special file; if yes, then the condition becomes true.	[-f $file] is true.

-g file	Checks if file has its set group ID (SGID) bit set; if yes, then the condition becomes true.	[-g $file] is false.
-k file	Checks if file has its sticky bit set; if yes, then the condition becomes true.	[-k $file] is false.
-p file	Checks if file is a named pipe; if yes, then the condition becomes true.	[-p $file] is false.
-t file	Checks if file descriptor is open and associated with a terminal; if yes, then the condition becomes true.	[-t $file] is false.
-u file	Checks if file has its Set User ID (SUID) bit set; if yes, then the condition becomes true.	[-u $file] is false.
-r file	Checks if file is readable; if yes, then the condition becomes true.	[-r $file] is true.
-w file	Checks if file is writable; if yes, then the condition becomes true.	[-w $file] is true.
-x file	Checks if file is executable; if yes, then the condition becomes true.	[-x $file] is true.

-s file	Checks if file has size greater than 0; if yes, then condition becomes true.	[-s $file] is true.
-e file	Checks if file exists; is true even if file is a directory but exists.	[-e $file] is true.

C Shell Operators

Following will give you a brief idea on C Shell Operators –

We will now list down all the operators available in C Shell. Here most of the operators are very similar to what we have in C Programming language.

Operators are listed in the order of decreasing precedence –

Arithmetic and Logical Operators

The following table lists out a few Arithmetic and Logical Operators –

S.No.	Operator & Description
1	**( )** Change precedence
2	**~** 1's complement
3	**!**

		Logical negation
4	*****	Multiply
5	**/**	Divide
6	**%**	Modulo
7	**+**	Add
8	**-**	Subtract
9	**<<**	Left shift
10	**>>**	Right shift
11	**==**	String comparison for equality
12	**!=**	

	String comparison for non equality
13	**=~** Pattern matching
14	**&** Bitwise "and"
15	**^** Bitwise "exclusive or"
16	**|** Bitwise "inclusive or"
17	**&&** Logical "and"
18	**||** Logical "or"
19	**++** Increment
20	**--** Decrement
21	**=**

	Assignment	
22	***=** Multiply left side by right side and update left side	
23	**/=** Divide left side by right side and update left side	
24	**+=** Add left side to right side and update left side	
25	**-=** Subtract left side from right side and update left side	
26	**^=** "Exclusive or" left side to right side and update left side	
27	**%=** Divide left by right side and update left side with remainder	

File Test Operators

The following operators test various properties associated with a Unix file.

S.No.	Operator & Description
1	**-r file** Checks if file is readable; if yes, then the condition becomes true.
2	**-w file** Checks if file is writable; if yes, then the condition becomes true.
3	**-x file** Checks if file is executable; if yes, then the condition becomes true.
4	**-f file** Checks if file is an ordinary file as opposed to a directory or special file; if yes, then the condition becomes true.
5	**-z file** Checks if file has size greater than 0; if yes, then the condition becomes true.

6	**-d file**
	Checks if file is a directory; if yes, then the condition becomes true.
7	**-e file**
	Checks if file exists; is true even if file is a directory but exists.
8	**-o file**
	Checks if user owns the file; returns true if the user is the owner of the file.

Korn Shell Operators

Following helps you understand Korn Shell Operators –

We will now discuss all the operators available in Korn Shell. Most of the operators are very similar to what we have in the C Programming language.

Operators are listed in the order of decreasing precedence –

Arithmatic and Logical Operators

S.No.	Operator & Description
1	**+** Unary plus
2	**-** Unary minus
3	**!~** Logical negation; binary inversion (one's complement)
4	***** Multiply

5	/ Divide
6	**%** Modulo
7	**+** Add
8	**-** Subtract
9	**<<** Left shift
10	**>>** Right shift
11	**==** String comparison for equality
12	**!=** String comparison for non-equality
13	**=~**

	Pattern matching
14	**&** Bitwise "and"
15	**^** Bitwise "exclusive or"
16	**|** Bitwise "inclusive or"
17	**&&** Logical "and"
18	**||** Logical "or"
19	**++** Increment
20	**--** Decrement
21	**=** Assignment

File Test Operators

Following operators test various properties associated with a Unix file.

S.No.	Operator & Description
1	**-r file** Checks if file is readable; if yes, then the condition becomes true.
2	**-w file** Checks if file is writable; if yes, then the condition becomes true.
3	**-x file** Checks if file is executable; if yes, then the condition becomes true.
4	**-f file** Checks if file is an ordinary file as opposed to a directory or special file; if yes, then the condition becomes true.
5	**-s file** Checks if file has size greater than 0; if yes, then the condition becomes true.

6	**-d file**
	Checks if file is a directory; if yes, then the condition becomes true.
7	**-e file**
	Checks if file exists; is true even if file is a directory but exists.

Unix - Shell Decision Making

In this chapter, we will understand shell decision-making in Unix. While writing a shell script, there may be a situation when you need to adopt one path out of the given two paths. So you need to make use of conditional statements that allow your program to make correct decisions and perform the right actions.

Unix Shell supports conditional statements which are used to perform different actions based on different conditions. We will now understand two decision-making statements here —

- The if...else statement
- The case...esac statement

The if...else statements

If else statements are useful decision-making statements which can be used to select an option from a given set of options.

Unix Shell supports following forms of if...else statement —

if...fi statement

The **if...fi** statement is the fundamental control statement that allows Shell to make decisions and execute statements conditionally.

Syntax

```
if [ expression ]
then
    Statement(s) to be executed if expression is true
fi
```

The *Shell expression* is evaluated in the above syntax. If the resulting value is *true*, given *statement(s)* are executed. If the *expression* is *false* then no statement would be executed. Most of the times, comparison operators are used for making decisions.

It is recommended to be careful with the spaces between braces and expression. No space produces a syntax error.

If **expression** is a shell command, then it will be assumed true if it returns **0** after execution. If it is a Boolean expression, then it would be true if it returns true.

Example

```
#!/bin/sh

a=10

b=20

if [ $a == $b ]

then

    echo "a is equal to b"

fi

if [ $a != $b ]

then

    echo "a is not equal to b"

fi
```

The above script will generate the following result —

```
a is not equal to b
```

if...else...fi statement

The **if...else...fi** statement is the next form of control statement that allows Shell to execute statements in a controlled way and make the right choice.

Syntax

```
if [ expression ]
then
   Statement(s) to be executed if expression is true
else
   Statement(s) to be executed if expression is not true
fi
```

The Shell *expression* is evaluated in the above syntax. If the resulting value is *true*, given *statement(s)* are executed. If the *expression* is *false*, then no statement will be executed.

Example

The above example can also be written using the *if...else* statement as follows –

```
#!/bin/sh

a=10

b=20

if [ $a == $b ]

then

   echo "a is equal to b"

else

   echo "a is not equal to b"

fi
```

Upon execution, you will receive the following result –

```
a is not equal to b
```

if...elif...else...fi statement

The **if...elif...fi** statement is the one level advance form of control statement that allows Shell to make correct decision out of several conditions.

Syntax

```
if [ expression 1 ]
then
    Statement(s) to be executed if expression 1 is true
elif [ expression 2 ]
then
    Statement(s) to be executed if expression 2 is true
elif [ expression 3 ]
then
    Statement(s) to be executed if expression 3 is true
else
    Statement(s) to be executed if no expression is true
fi
```

This code is just a series of *if* statements, where each *if* is part of the *else*clause of the previous statement. Here statement(s) are executed based on the true condition, if none of the condition is true then *else* block is executed.

Example

```
#!/bin/sh

a=10

b=20

if [ $a == $b ]
```

```
then

    echo "a is equal to b"

elif [ $a -gt $b ]

then

    echo "a is greater than b"

elif [ $a -lt $b ]

then

    echo "a is less than b"

else

    echo "None of the condition met"

fi
```

Upon execution, you will receive the following result —

```
a is less than b
```

Most of the if statements check relations using relational operators discussed in the previous chapter.

The case...esac Statement

You can use multiple if...elif statements to perform a multiway branch. However, this is not always the best solution, especially when all of the branches depend on the value of a single variable.

Unix Shell supports case...esac statement which handles exactly this situation, and it does so more efficiently than repeated if...elif statements.

There is only one form of case...esac statement which has been described in detail here −

case...esac statement

You can use multiple **if...elif** statements to perform a multiway branch. However, this is not always the best solution, especially when all of the branches depend on the value of a single variable.

Shell supports **case...esac** statement which handles exactly this situation, and it does so more efficiently than repeated if...elif statements.

Syntax

The basic syntax of the **case...esac** statement is to give an expression to evaluate and to execute several different statements based on the value of the expression.

The interpreter checks each case against the value of the expression until a match is found. If nothing matches, a default condition will be used.

```
case word in
   pattern1)
      Statement(s) to be executed if pattern1 matches
      ;;
   pattern2)
      Statement(s) to be executed if pattern2 matches
      ;;
   pattern3)
      Statement(s) to be executed if pattern3 matches
      ;;
   *)
      Default condition to be executed
      ;;
esac
```

Here the string word is compared against every pattern until a match is found. The statement(s) following the matching pattern executes. If no matches are found, the case statement exits without performing any action.

There is no maximum number of patterns, but the minimum is one.

When statement(s) part executes, the command ;; indicates that the program flow should jump to the end of the entire case statement. This is similar to break in the C programming language.

Example

```
#!/bin/sh

FRUIT="kiwi"

case "$FRUIT" in

   "apple") echo "Apple pie is quite tasty."

   ;;

   "banana") echo "I like banana nut bread."

   ;;

   "kiwi") echo "New Zealand is famous for kiwi."

   ;;

esac
```

Upon execution, you will receive the following result —

```
New Zealand is famous for kiwi.
```

A good use for a case statement is the evaluation of command line arguments as follows —

```
#!/bin/sh


option="${1}"

case ${option} in

   -f) FILE="${2}"

      echo "File name is $FILE"
```

```
    ;;

  -d) DIR="${2}"

     echo "Dir name is $DIR"

     ;;

  *)

     echo "`basename ${0}`:usage: [-f file] | [-d
directory]"

     exit 1 # Command to come out of the program with
status 1

     ;;

esac
```

Here is a sample run of the above program –

```
$./test.sh
test.sh: usage: [ -f filename ] | [ -d directory ]
$ ./test.sh -f index.htm
$ vi test.sh
$ ./test.sh -f index.htm
File name is index.htm
$ ./test.sh -d unix
Dir name is unix
$
```

The case...esac statement in the Unix shell is very similar to the switch...case statement we have in other programming languages like C or C++ and PERL, etc.

Unix - Shell Loop Types

In this chapter, we will discuss shell loops in Unix. A loop is a powerful programming tool that enables you to execute a set of commands repeatedly. In this chapter, we will examine the following types of loops available to shell programmers −

The while loop

The **while** loop enables you to execute a set of commands repeatedly until some condition occurs. It is usually used when you need to manipulate the value of a variable repeatedly.

Syntax

```
while command
do
    Statement(s) to be executed if command is true
done
```

Here the Shell *command* is evaluated. If the resulting value is *true*, given *statement(s)* are executed.

If *command* is *false* then no statement will be executed and the program will jump to the next line after the done statement.

Example

Here is a simple example that uses the **while** loop to display the numbers zero to nine —

```
#!/bin/sh

a=0

while [ $a -lt 10 ]

do

   echo $a

    a=`expr $a + 1`

done
```

Upon execution, you will receive the following result —

```
0
1
2
3
4
5
6
7
8
9
```

Each time this loop executes, the variable **a** is checked to see whether it has a value that is less than 10. If the value of **a** is less than 10, this test condition has an exit status of 0. In this case, the current value of **a** is displayed and later **a** is incremented by 1.

The for loop

The **for** loop operates on lists of items. It repeats a set of commands for every item in a list.

Syntax

```
for var in word1 word2 ... wordN
do
    Statement(s) to be executed for every word.
done
```

Here *var* is the name of a variable and word1 to wordN are sequences of characters separated by spaces (words). Each time the for loop executes, the value of the variable var is set to the next word in the list of words, word1 to wordN.

Example

Here is a simple example that uses the **for** loop to span through the given list of numbers —

```
#!/bin/sh

for var in 0 1 2 3 4 5 6 7 8 9

do

    echo $var

done
```

Upon execution, you will receive the following result −

```
0
1
2
3
4
5
6
7
8
9
```

Following is the example to display all the files starting with **.bash** and available in your home. We will execute this script from my root −

```
#!/bin/sh

for FILE in $HOME/.bash*

do

    echo $FILE

done
```

The above script will produce the following result −

```
/root/.bash_history
/root/.bash_logout
/root/.bash_profile
/root/.bashrc
```

The until loop

The while loop is perfect for a situation where you need to execute a set of commands while some condition is true. Sometimes you need to execute a set of commands until a condition is true.

Syntax

```
until command
do
     Statement(s) to be executed until command is true
done
```

Here the Shell *command* is evaluated. If the resulting value is *false*, given *statement(s)* are executed. If the *command* is *true* then no statement will be executed and the program jumps to the next line after the done statement.

Example

Here is a simple example that uses the until loop to display the numbers zero to nine –

```
#!/bin/sh

a=0

until [ ! $a -lt 10 ]

do

    echo $a

    a = `expr $a + 1`

done
```

Upon execution, you will receive the following result –

```
0
1
2
3
4
5
6
7
8
9
```

The select loop

The **select** loop provides an easy way to create a numbered menu from which users can select options. It is useful when you need to ask the user to choose one or more items from a list of choices.

Syntax

```
select var in word1 word2 ... wordN
do
    Statement(s) to be executed for every word.
done
```

Here *var* is the name of a variable and **word1** to **wordN** are sequences of characters separated by spaces (words). Each time the **for** loop executes, the value of the variable var is set to the next word in the list of words, **word1** to **wordN**.

For every selection, a set of commands will be executed within the loop. This loop was introduced in **ksh** and has been adapted into bash. It is not available in **sh**.

Example

Here is a simple example to let the user select a drink of choice —

```
#!/bin/ksh

select DRINK in tea cofee water juice appe all
none
```

```
    do

        case $DRINK in

            tea|cofee|water|all)

                echo "Go to canteen"

                ;;

            juice|appe)

                echo "Available at home"

            ;;

            none)

                break

            ;;

            *) echo "ERROR: Invalid selection"

            ;;

        esac

    done
```

The menu presented by the select loop looks like the following –

```
$./test.sh
1) tea
2) cofee
3) water
4) juice
5) appe
6) all
7) none
#? juice
Available at home
```

```
#? none
$
```

You can change the prompt displayed by the select loop by altering the variable PS3 as follows −

```
$PS3 = "Please make a selection => " ; export PS3
$./test.sh
1) tea
2) cofee
3) water
4) juice
5) appe
6) all
7) none
Please make a selection => juice
Available at home
Please make a selection => none
$
```

You will use different loops based on the situation. For example, the whileloop executes the given commands until the given condition remains true; the until loop executes until a given condition becomes true.

Once you have good programming practice you will gain the expertise and thereby, start using appropriate loop based on the situation. Here, while and for loops are available in most of the other programming languages like C, C++ and PERL, etc.

Nesting Loops

All the loops support nesting concept which means you can put one loop inside another similar one or different loops. This nesting can go up to unlimited number of times based on your requirement.

Here is an example of nesting while loop. The other loops can be nested based on the programming requirement in a similar way —

Nesting while Loops

It is possible to use a while loop as part of the body of another while loop.

Syntax

```
while command1 ; # this is loop1, the outer loop
do
   Statement(s) to be executed if command1 is true

   while command2 ; # this is loop2, the inner loop
   do
      Statement(s) to be executed if command2 is true
   done

   Statement(s) to be executed if command1 is true
done
```

Example

Here is a simple example of loop nesting. Let's add another countdown loop inside the loop that you used to count to nine —

```
#!/bin/sh

a=0
while [ "$a" -lt 10 ]   # this is loop1
do
   b="$a"
   while [ "$b" -ge 0 ] # this is loop2
   do
      echo -n "$b "
```

```
    b=`expr $b - 1`
  done
  echo
  a=`expr $a + 1`
done
```

This will produce the following result. It is important to note how echo -nworks here. Here -n option lets echo avoid printing a new line character.

```
0
1 0
2 1 0
3 2 1 0
4 3 2 1 0
5 4 3 2 1 0
6 5 4 3 2 1 0
7 6 5 4 3 2 1 0
8 7 6 5 4 3 2 1 0
9 8 7 6 5 4 3 2 1 0
```

Unix - Shell Loop Control

In this chapter, we will discuss shell loop control in Unix. So far you have looked at creating loops and working with loops to accomplish different tasks. Sometimes you need to stop a loop or skip iterations of the loop.

In this chapter, we will learn following two statements that are used to control shell loops—

- The break statement
- The continue statement

The infinite Loop

All the loops have a limited life and they come out once the condition is false or true depending on the loop.

A loop may continue forever if the required condition is not met. A loop that executes forever without terminating executes for an infinite number of times. For this reason, such loops are called infinite loops.

Example

Here is a simple example that uses the while loop to display the numbers zero to nine —

```
#!/bin/sh

a=10

until [ $a -lt 10 ]
do
   echo $a
```

```
   a=expr $a + 1`
done
```

This loop continues forever because a is always greater than or equal to 10and it is never less than 10.

The break Statement

The break statement is used to terminate the execution of the entire loop, after completing the execution of all of the lines of code up to the break statement. It then steps down to the code following the end of the loop.

Syntax

The following break statement is used to come out of a loop −

```
break
```

The break command can also be used to exit from a nested loop using this format −

```
break n
```

Here n specifies the nth enclosing loop to the exit from.

Example

Here is a simple example which shows that loop terminates as soon as abecomes 5 −

```
#!/bin/sh

a=0

while [ $a -lt 10 ]
```

```
do
   echo $a
   if [ $a -eq 5 ]
   then
      break
   fi
   a=`expr $a + 1`
done
```

Upon execution, you will receive the following result −

```
0
1
2
3
4
5
```

Here is a simple example of nested for loop. This script breaks out of both loops if var1 equals 2 and var2 equals 0 −

```
#!/bin/sh

for var1 in 1 2 3
do
   for var2 in 0 5
   do
      if [ $var1 -eq 2 -a $var2 -eq 0 ]
      then
         break 2
      else
         echo "$var1 $var2"
      fi
   done
done
```

Upon execution, you will receive the following result. In the inner loop, you have a break command with the argument 2. This indicates that if a condition is met you should break out of outer loop and ultimately from the inner loop as well.

```
1 0
1 5
```

The continue statement

The continue statement is similar to the break command, except that it causes the current iteration of the loop to exit, rather than the entire loop.

This statement is useful when an error has occurred but you want to try to execute the next iteration of the loop.

Syntax

```
continue
```

Like with the break statement, an integer argument can be given to the continue command to skip commands from nested loops.

```
continue n
```

Here n specifies the nth enclosing loop to continue from.

Example

The following loop makes use of the continue statement which returns from the continue statement and starts processing the next statement —

```
#!/bin/sh

NUMS="1 2 3 4 5 6 7"
```

```
for NUM in $NUMS
do
   Q=`expr $NUM % 2`
   if [ $Q -eq 0 ]
   then
      echo "Number is an even number!!"
      continue
   fi
   echo "Found odd number"
done
```

Upon execution, you will receive the following result —

```
Found odd number
Number is an even number!!
Found odd number
Number is an even number!!
Found odd number
Number is an even number!!
Found odd number
```

Unix - Shell Substitution

What is Substitution?

The shell performs substitution when it encounters an expression that contains one or more special characters.

Example

Here, the printing value of the variable is substituted by its value. Same time, "\n" is substituted by a new line —

```
#!/bin/sh

a=10
echo -e "Value of a is $a \n"
```

You will receive the following result. Here the -e option enables the interpretation of backslash escapes.

```
Value of a is 10
```

Following is the result without -e option —

```
Value of a is 10\n
```

Here are following escape sequences which can be used in echo command –

S.No.	Escape & Description
1	\\ backslash
2	\a alert (BEL)
3	\b backspace
4	\c suppress trailing newline
5	\f form feed

6	\n	new line
7	\r	carriage return
8	\t	horizontal tab
9	\v	vertical tab

You can use the -E option to disable the interpretation of the backslash escapes (default).

You can use the -n option to disable the insertion of a new line.

Command Substitution

Command substitution is the mechanism by which the shell performs a given set of commands and then substitutes their output in the place of the commands.

Syntax

The command substitution is performed when a command is given as −

`` `command` ``

When performing the command substitution make sure that you use the backquote, not the single quote character.

Example

Command substitution is generally used to assign the output of a command to a variable. Each of the following examples demonstrates the command substitution −

```
#!/bin/sh

DATE=`date`
echo "Date is $DATE"

USERS=`who | wc -l`
echo "Logged in user are $USERS"

UP=`date ; uptime`
echo "Uptime is $UP"
```

Upon execution, you will receive the following result −

```
Date is Thu Jul  2 03:59:57 MST 2009
Logged in user are 1
Uptime is Thu Jul  2 03:59:57 MST 2009
03:59:57 up 20 days, 14:03,  1 user,  load avg: 0.13, 0.07, 0.15
```

Variable Substitution

Variable substitution enables the shell programmer to manipulate the value of a variable based on its state.

Here is the following table for all the possible substitutions —

S.No.	Form & Description
1	${var} Substitute the value of *var*.
2	${var:-word} If *var* is null or unset, *word* is substituted for var. The value of *var*does not change.
3	${var:=word} If *var* is null or unset, *var* is set to the value of word.

| 4 | ${var:?message}

If *var* is null or unset, *message* is printed to standard error. This checks that variables are set correctly. |

| 5 | ${var:+word}

If *var* is set, *word* is substituted for var. The value of *var* does not change. |

Example

Following is the example to show various states of the above substitution —

```
#!/bin/sh

echo ${var:-"Variable is not set"}
echo "1 - Value of var is ${var}"

echo ${var:="Variable is not set"}
echo "2 - Value of var is ${var}"

unset var
echo ${var:+"This is default value"}
echo "3 - Value of var is $var"

var="Prefix"
echo ${var:+"This is default value"}
echo "4 - Value of var is $var"
```

```
echo ${var:?"Print this message"}
echo "5 - Value of var is ${var}"
```

Upon execution, you will receive the following result −

```
Variable is not set
1 - Value of var is
Variable is not set
2 - Value of var is Variable is not set

3 - Value of var is
This is default value
4 - Value of var is Prefix
Prefix
5 - Value of var is Prefix
```

Unix - Shell Quoting Mechanisms

In this chapter, we will discuss in detail about the Shell quoting mechanisms. We will start by discussing the metacharacters.

The Metacharacters

Unix Shell provides various metacharacters which have special meaning while using them in any Shell Script and causes termination of a word unless quoted.

For example, ? matches with a single character while listing files in a directory and an * matches more than one character. Here is a list of most of the shell special characters (also called metacharacters) −

* ? [ ] ' " \ $; & ( ) | ^ < > new-line space tab

A character may be quoted (i.e., made to stand for itself) by preceding it with a \.

Example

Following example shows how to print a * or a ? −

#!/bin/sh

echo Hello; Word

Upon execution, you will receive the following result —

Hello
./test.sh: line 2: Word: command not found

shell returned 127

Let us now try using a quoted character —

#!/bin/sh

echo Hello\; Word

Upon execution, you will receive the following result —

Hello; Word

The $ sign is one of the metacharacters, so it must be quoted to avoid special handling by the shell —

#!/bin/sh

echo "I have \$1200"

Upon execution, you will receive the following result —

I have $1200

The following table lists the four forms of quoting −

S.No.	Quoting & Description
1	Single quote All special characters between these quotes lose their special meaning.
2	Double quote Most special characters between these quotes lose their special meaning with these exceptions − • $ • ` • \\$ • \\' • \\" • \\\\
3	Backslash Any character immediately following the backslash loses its special meaning.

4	Back quote
	Anything in between back quotes would be treated as a command and would be executed.

The Single Quotes

Consider an echo command that contains many special shell characters —

```
echo <-$1500.**>; (update?) [y|n]
```

Putting a backslash in front of each special character is tedious and makes the line difficult to read —

```
echo \<-\$1500.\*\*\>\; \(update\?\) \[y\|n\]
```

There is an easy way to quote a large group of characters. Put a single quote (') at the beginning and at the end of the string —

```
echo '<-$1500.**>; (update?) [y|n]'
```

Characters within single quotes are quoted just as if a backslash is in front of each character. With this, the echo command displays in a proper way.

If a single quote appears within a string to be output, you should not put the whole string within single quotes instead you should precede that using a backslash (\) as follows —

```
echo 'It\'s Shell Programming'
```

The Double Quotes

Try to execute the following shell script. This shell script makes use of single quote −

```
VAR=ZARA
echo '$VAR owes <-$1500.**>; [ as of (`date +%m/%d`) ]'
```

Upon execution, you will receive the following result −

```
$VAR owes <-$1500.**>; [ as of (`date +%m/%d`) ]
```

This is not what had to be displayed. It is obvious that single quotes prevent variable substitution. If you want to substitute variable values and to make inverted commas work as expected, then you would need to put your commands in double quotes as follows −

```
VAR=ZARA
echo "$VAR owes <-\$1500.**>; [ as of (`date +%m/%d`) ]"
```

Upon execution, you will receive the following result −

```
ZARA owes <-$1500.**>; [ as of (07/02) ]
```

Double quotes take away the special meaning of all characters except the following −

- $ for parameter substitution
- Backquotes for command substitution
- \$ to enable literal dollar signs
- \` to enable literal backquotes
- \" to enable embedded double quotes
- \\ to enable embedded backslashes
- All other \ characters are literal (not special)

Characters within single quotes are quoted just as if a backslash is in front of each character. This helps the echo command display properly.

If a single quote appears within a string to be output, you should not put the whole string within single quotes instead you should precede that using a backslash (\) as follows —

```
echo 'It\'s Shell Programming'
```

The Backquotes

Putting any Shell command in between backquotes executes the command.

Syntax

Here is the simple syntax to put any Shell command in between backquotes —

Syntax

```
var = `command`
```

Example

The date command is executed in the following example and the produced result is stored in DATA variable.

```
DATE=`date`
```

```
echo "Current Date: $DATE"
```

Upon execution, you will receive the following result —

```
Current Date: Thu Jul  2 05:28:45 MST 2009
```

Unix - Shell Input/Output Redirections

In this chapter, we will discuss in detail about the Shell input/output redirections. Most Unix system commands take input from your terminal and send the resulting output back to your terminal. A command normally reads its input from the standard input, which happens to be your terminal by default. Similarly, a command normally writes its output to standard output, which is again your terminal by default.

Output Redirection

The output from a command normally intended for standard output can be easily diverted to a file instead. This capability is known as output redirection.

If the notation > file is appended to any command that normally writes its output to standard output, the output of that command will be written to file instead of your terminal.

Check the following who command which redirects the complete output of the command in the users file.

```
$ who > users
```

Notice that no output appears at the terminal. This is because the output has been redirected from the default standard output device (the terminal) into the specified file. You can check the users file for the complete content —

```
$ cat users
oko       tty01  Sep 12 07:30
ai        tty15  Sep 12 13:32
ruth      tty21  Sep 12 10:10
pat       tty24  Sep 12 13:07
```

```
steve      tty25  Sep 12 13:03
$
```

If a command has its output redirected to a file and the file already contains some data, that data will be lost. Consider the following example —

```
$ echo line 1 > users
$ cat users
line 1
$
```

You can use >> operator to append the output in an existing file as follows —

```
$ echo line 2 >> users
$ cat users
line 1
line 2
$
```

Input Redirection

Just as the output of a command can be redirected to a file, so can the input of a command be redirected from a file. As the greater-than character > is used for output redirection, the less-than character < is used to redirect the input of a command.

The commands that normally take their input from the standard input can have their input redirected from a file in this manner. For example, to count the number of lines in the file *users* generated above, you can execute the command as follows —

```
$ wc -l users
2 users
$
```

- 180 -

Upon execution, you will receive the following output. You can count the number of lines in the file by redirecting the standard input of the wccommand from the file *users* −

```
$ wc -l < users
2
$
```

Note that there is a difference in the output produced by the two forms of the wc command. In the first case, the name of the file users is listed with the line count; in the second case, it is not.

In the first case, wc knows that it is reading its input from the file users. In the second case, it only knows that it is reading its input from standard input so it does not display file name.

Here Document

A here document is used to redirect input into an interactive shell script or program.

We can run an interactive program within a shell script without user action by supplying the required input for the interactive program, or interactive shell script.

The general form for a here document is −

```
command << delimiter
document
delimiter
```

Here the shell interprets the << operator as an instruction to read input until it finds a line containing the specified delimiter. All the input lines up to the line containing the delimiter are then fed into the standard input of the command.

The delimiter tells the shell that the here document has completed. Without it, the shell continues to read the input forever. The delimiter must be a single word that does not contain spaces or tabs.

Following is the input to the command wc -l to count the total number of lines —

```
$wc -l << EOF
    This is a simple lookup program
        for good (and bad) restaurants
        in Cape Town.
EOF
3
$
```

You can use the here document to print multiple lines using your script as follows —

```
#!/bin/sh

cat << EOF
This is a simple lookup program
for good (and bad) restaurants
in Cape Town.
EOF
```

Upon execution, you will receive the following result —

```
This is a simple lookup program
for good (and bad) restaurants
in Cape Town.
```

The following script runs a session with the vi text editor and saves the input in the file test.txt.

```
#!/bin/sh

filename=test.txt
vi $filename <<EndOfCommands
```

i
This file was created automatically from
a shell script
^[
ZZ
EndOfCommands

If you run this script with vim acting as vi, then you will likely see output like the following —

```
$ sh test.sh
Vim: Warning: Input is not from a terminal
$
```

After running the script, you should see the following added to the file test.txt—

```
$ cat test.txt
This file was created automatically from
a shell script
$
```

Discard the output

Sometimes you will need to execute a command, but you don't want the output displayed on the screen. In such cases, you can discard the output by redirecting it to the file /dev/null —

```
$ command > /dev/null
```

Here command is the name of the command you want to execute. The file /dev/null is a special file that automatically discards all its input.

To discard both output of a command and its error output, use standard redirection to redirect STDERR to STDOUT —

```
$ command > /dev/null 2>&1
```

Here 2 represents STDERR and 1 represents STDOUT. You can display a message on to STDERR by redirecting STDOUT into STDERR as follows —

```
$ echo message 1>&2
```

Redirection Commands

Following is a complete list of commands which you can use for redirection —

S.No.	Command & Description
1	pgm > file Output of pgm is redirected to file
2	pgm < file Program pgm reads its input from file
3	pgm >> file Output of pgm is appended to file

4	n > file
	Output from stream with descriptor n redirected to file
5	n >> file
	Output from stream with descriptor n appended to file
6	n >& m
	Merges output from stream n with stream m
7	n <& m
	Merges input from stream n with stream m
8	<< tag
	Standard input comes from here through next tag at the start of line

9		
	Takes output from one program, or process, and sends it to another	

Note that the file descriptor 0 is normally standard input (STDIN), 1 is standard output (STDOUT), and 2 is standard error output (STDERR).

Unix - Shell Functions

In this chapter, we will discuss in detail about the shell functions. Functions enable you to break down the overall functionality of a script into smaller, logical subsections, which can then be called upon to perform their individual tasks when needed.

Using functions to perform repetitive tasks is an excellent way to create code reuse. This is an important part of modern object-oriented programming principles.

Shell functions are similar to subroutines, procedures, and functions in other programming languages.

Creating Functions

To declare a function, simply use the following syntax —

```
function_name () {
   list of commands
}
```

The name of your function is function_name, and that's what you will use to call it from elsewhere in your scripts. The function name must be followed by parentheses, followed by a list of commands enclosed within braces.

Example

Following example shows the use of function —

```sh
#!/bin/sh

# Define your function here
Hello () {
   echo "Hello World"
}

# Invoke your function
Hello
```

Upon execution, you will receive the following output —

```
$./test.sh
Hello World
```

Pass Parameters to a Function

You can define a function that will accept parameters while calling the function. These parameters would be represented by $1, $2 and so on.

Following is an example where we pass two parameters *Zara* and *Ali* and then we capture and print these parameters in the function.

```sh
#!/bin/sh

# Define your function here
Hello () {
   echo "Hello World $1 $2"
}
```

```
# Invoke your function
Hello Zara Ali
```

Upon execution, you will receive the following result —

```
$./test.sh
Hello World Zara Ali
```

Returning Values from Functions

If you execute an exit command from inside a function, its effect is not only to terminate execution of the function but also of the shell program that called the function.

If you instead want to just terminate execution of the function, then there is way to come out of a defined function.

Based on the situation you can return any value from your function using the return command whose syntax is as follows —

```
return code
```

Here code can be anything you choose here, but obviously you should choose something that is meaningful or useful in the context of your script as a whole.

Example

Following function returns a value 1 —

```
#!/bin/sh

# Define your function here
Hello () {
   echo "Hello World $1 $2"
   return 10
}

# Invoke your function
Hello Zara Ali

# Capture value returnd by last command
ret=$?

echo "Return value is $ret"
```

Upon execution, you will receive the following result —

```
$./test.sh
Hello World Zara Ali
Return value is 10
```

Nested Functions

One of the more interesting features of functions is that they can call themselves and also other functions. A function that calls itself is known as a *recursive function*.

Following example demonstrates nesting of two functions —

```
#!/bin/sh

# Calling one function from another
```

```
number_one () {
   echo "This is the first function speaking..."
   number_two
}

number_two () {
   echo "This is now the second function speaking..."
}

# Calling function one.
number_one
```

Upon execution, you will receive the following result −

```
This is the first function speaking...
This is now the second function speaking...
```

Function Call from Prompt

You can put definitions for commonly used functions inside your *.profile*. These definitions will be available whenever you log in and you can use them at the command prompt.

Alternatively, you can group the definitions in a file, say *test.sh*, and then execute the file in the current shell by typing −

```
$. test.sh
```

This has the effect of causing functions defined inside *test.sh* to be read and defined to the current shell as follows –

```
$ number_one
This is the first function speaking...
This is now the second function speaking...
$
```

To remove the definition of a function from the shell, use the unset command with the .f option. This command is also used to remove the definition of a variable to the shell.

```
$unset .f function_name
```

Unix - Shell Manpage Help

All the Unix commands come with a number of optional and mandatory options. It is very common to forget the complete syntax of these commands.

Because no one can possibly remember every Unix command and all its options, we have online help available to mitigate this right from when Unix was at its development stage.

Unix's version of Help files are called man pages. If there is a command name and you are not sure how to use it, then Man Pages help you out with every step.

Syntax

Here is the simple command that helps you get the detail of any Unix command while working with the system −

$man command

Example

Suppose there is a command that requires you to get help; assume that you want to know about pwd then you simply need to use the following command −

$man pwd

The above command helps you with the complete information about the pwdcommand. Try it yourself at your command prompt to get more detail.

You can get complete detail on man command itself using the following command —

$man man

Man Page Sections

Man pages are generally divided into sections, which generally vary by the man page author's preference. Following table lists some common sections —

S.No.	Section & Description
1	NAME Name of the command
2	SYNOPSIS General usage parameters of the command
3	DESCRIPTION Describes what the command does

4	OPTIONS
	Describes all the arguments or options to the command

5	SEE ALSO
	Lists other commands that are directly related to the command in the man page or closely resemble its functionality

6	BUGS
	Explains any known issues or bugs that exist with the command or its output

7	EXAMPLES
	Common usage examples that give the reader an idea of how the command can be used

8	AUTHORS
	The author of the man page/command

To sum it up, man pages are a vital resource and the first avenue of research when you need information about commands or files in a Unix system.

Useful Shell Commands

The following link gives you a list of the most important and very frequently used Unix Shell commands.

If you do not know how to use any command, then use man page to get complete detail about the command.

Here is the list of Unix Shell - Useful Commands

This quick guide lists commands, including a syntax and a brief description. For more detail, use —

```
$man command
```

Files and Directories

These commands allow you to create directories and handle files.

Given below is the list of commands in Files and Directories.

S.No.	Command & Description
1	**cat** Displays File Contents
2	**cd**

		Changes Directory to dirname
3	**chgrp**	Changes file group
4	**chmod**	Changes permissions
5	**cp**	Copies source file into destination
6	**file**	Determines file type
7	**find**	Finds files
8	**grep**	Searches files for regular expressions
9	**head**	Displays first few lines of a file

10	**ln** Creates softlink on oldname
11	**ls** Displays information about file type
12	**mkdir** Creates a new directory dirname
13	**more** Displays data in paginated form
14	**mv** Moves (Renames) an oldname to newname
15	**pwd** Prints current working directory
16	**rm** Removes (Deletes) filename
17	**rmdir**

	Deletes an existing directory provided it is empty
18	**tail** Prints last few lines in a file
19	**touch** Updates access and modification time of a file

Manipulating data

The contents of files can be compared and altered with the following commands.

Given below is the list of commands in Manipulating data.

S.No.	Command & Description
1	**awk** Pattern scanning and processing language
2	**cmp** Compares the contents of two files
3	**comm** Compares sorted data

4	**cut**
	Cuts out selected fields of each line of a file
5	**diff**
	Differential file comparator
6	**expand**
	Expands tabs to spaces
7	**join**
	Joins files on some common field
8	**perl**
	Data manipulation language
9	**sed**
	Stream text editor
10	**sort**
	Sorts file data
11	**split**

		Splits file into smaller files
12	**tr**	Translates characters
13	**uniq**	Reports repeated lines in a file
14	**wc**	Counts words, lines, and characters
15	**vi**	Opens vi text editor
16	**vim**	Opens vim text editor
17	**fmt**	Simple text formatter
18	**spell**	Checks text for spelling error

S.No.	Command & Description
19	**ispell** Checks text for spelling error
20	**emacs** GNU project Emacs
21	**ex, edit** Line editor
22	**emacs** GNU project Emacs

Compressed Files

Files may be compressed to save space. Compressed files can be created and examined.

S.No.	Command & Description
1	**compress** Compresses files
2	**gunzip**

	Helps uncompress gzipped files
3	**gzip** GNU alternative compression method
4	**uncompress** Helps uncompress files
5	**unzip** List, test and extract compressed files in a ZIP archive
6	**zcat** Cat a compressed file
7	**zcmp** Compares compressed files
8	**zdiff** Compares compressed files
9	**zmore** File perusal filter for crt viewing of compressed text

Getting Information

Various Unix manuals and documentation are available on-line. The following Shell commands give information —

S.No.	Command & Description
1	**apropos** Locates commands by keyword lookup
2	**info** Displays command information pages online
2	**man** Displays manual pages online
3	**whatis** Searches the whatis database for complete words
4	**yelp** GNOME help viewer

Network Communication

These following commands are used to send and receive files from a local Unix hosts to the remote host around the world.

S.No.	Command & Description
1	**ftp** File transfer program
2	**rcp** Remote file copy
3	**rlogin** Remote login to a Unix host
4	**rsh** Remote shell
5	**tftp** Trivial file transfer program
6	**telnet** Makes terminal connection to another host

7	**ssh**
	Secures shell terminal or command connection
8	**scp**
	Secures shell remote file copy
9	**sftp**
	Secures shell file transfer program

Some of these commands may be restricted at your computer for security reasons.

Messages between Users

The Unix systems support on-screen messages to other users and world-wide electronic mail —

S.No.	Command & Description
1	**evolution**
	GUI mail handling tool on Linux
2	**mail**
	Simple send or read mail program

3	**mesg** Permits or denies messages
4	**parcel** Sends files to another user
5	**pine** Vdu-based mail utility
6	**talk** Talks to another user
7	**write** Writes message to another user

Programming Utilities

The following programming tools and languages are available based on what you have installed on your Unix.

Given below is the list of tools and languages in Programming Utilities.

S.No.	Command & Description
1	**dbx** Sun debugger
2	**gdb** GNU debugger
3	**make** Maintains program groups and compile programs
4	**nm** Prints program's name list
5	**size** Prints program's sizes
6	**strip**

	Removes symbol table and relocation bits
7	**cb** C program beautifier
8	**cc** ANSI C compiler for Suns SPARC systems
9	**ctrace** C program debugger
10	**gcc** GNU ANSI C Compiler
11	**indent** Indent and format C program source
12	**bc** Interactive arithmetic language processor
13	**gcl** GNU Common Lisp

14	**perl** General purpose language
15	**php** Web page embedded language
16	**py** Python language interpreter
17	**asp** Web page embedded language
18	**cc** C++ compiler for Suns SPARC systems
19	**g++** GNU C++ Compiler
20	**javac** JAVA compiler
21	**appletvieweir**

	JAVA applet viewer
22	**netbeans** Java integrated development environment on Linux
23	**sqlplus** Runs the Oracle SQL interpreter
24	**sqlldr** Runs the Oracle SQL data loader
25	**mysql** Runs the mysql SQL interpreter

Misc Commands

These commands list or alter information about the system —
Given below is the list of Misc Commands in Unix.

S.No.	Command & Description
1	**chfn** Changes your finger information
2	**chgrp** Changes the group ownership of a file
3	**chown** Changes owner
4	**date** Prints the date
5	**determin** Automatically finds terminal type
6	**du** Prints amount of disk usage

7	**echo**
	Echo arguments to the standard options
8	**exit**
	Quits the system
9	**finger**
	Prints information about logged-in users
10	**groupadd**
	Creates a user group
11	**groups**
	Show group memberships
12	**homequota**
	Shows quota and file usage
13	**iostat**
	Reports I/O statistics
14	**kill**

		Sends a signal to a process
15	**last**	
	Shows last logins of users	
16	**logout**	
	Logs off Unix	
17	**lun**	
	Lists user names or login ID	
18	**netstat**	
	Shows network status	
19	**passwd**	
	Changes user password	
20	**passwd**	
	Changes your login password	
21	**printenv**	
	Displays value of a shell variable	

22	**ps**
	Displays the status of current processes
23	**ps**
	Prints process status statistics
24	**quota -v**
	Displays disk usage and limits
25	**reset**
	Resets terminal mode
26	**script**
	Keeps script of terminal session
27	**script**
	Saves the output of a command or process
28	**setenv**
	Sets environment variables
30	**stty**

	Sets terminal options
31	**time** Helps time a command
32	**top** Displays all system processes
33	**tset** Sets terminal mode
34	**tty** Prints current terminal name
35	**umask** Show the permissions that are given to view files by default
36	**uname** Displays name of the current system
37	**uptime** Gets the system up time

38	**useradd** Creates a user account
39	**users** Prints names of logged in users
40	**vmstat** Reports virtual memory statistics
41	**w** Shows what logged in users are doing
42	**who** Lists logged in users

Unix - Regular Expressions with SED

In this chapter, we will discuss in detail about regular expressions with SED in Unix.

A regular expression is a string that can be used to describe several sequences of characters. Regular expressions are used by several different Unix commands, including ed, sed, awk, grep, and to a more limited extent, vi.

Here SED stands for stream editor. This stream-oriented editor was created exclusively for executing scripts. Thus, all the input you feed into it passes through and goes to STDOUT and it does not change the input file.

Invoking sed

Before we start, let us ensure we have a local copy of /etc/passwd text file to work with sed.

As mentioned previously, sed can be invoked by sending data through a pipe to it as follows —

```
$ cat /etc/passwd | sed
Usage: sed [OPTION]... {script-other-script} [input-file]...

 -n, --quiet, --silent
          suppress automatic printing of pattern space
 -e script, --expression = script
..........................
```

The cat command dumps the contents of /etc/passwd to sed through the pipe into sed's pattern space. The pattern space is the internal work buffer that sed uses for its operations.

The sed General Syntax

Following is the general syntax for sed −

/pattern/action

Here, pattern is a regular expression, and action is one of the commands given in the following table. If pattern is omitted, action is performed for every line as we have seen above.

The slash character (/) that surrounds the pattern are required because they are used as delimiters.

S.No.	Range & Description
1	p Prints the line
2	d Deletes the line
3	s/pattern1/pattern2/ Substitutes the first occurrence of pattern1 with pattern2

Deleting All Lines with sed

We will now understand how to delete all lines with sed. Invoke sed again; but the sed is now supposed to use the editing command delete line, denoted by the single letter d —

```
$ cat /etc/passwd | sed 'd'
$
```

Instead of invoking sed by sending a file to it through a pipe, the sed can be instructed to read the data from a file, as in the following example.

The following command does exactly the same as in the previous example, without the cat command —

```
$ sed -e 'd' /etc/passwd
$
```

The sed Addresses

The sed also supports addresses. Addresses are either particular locations in a file or a range where a particular editing command should be applied. When the sed encounters no addresses, it performs its operations on every line in the file.

The following command adds a basic address to the sed command you've been using —

```
$ cat /etc/passwd | sed '1d' |more
daemon:x:1:1:daemon:/usr/sbin:/bin/sh
bin:x:2:2:bin:/bin:/bin/sh
sys:x:3:3:sys:/dev:/bin/sh
sync:x:4:65534:sync:/bin:/bin/sync
games:x:5:60:games:/usr/games:/bin/sh
man:x:6:12:man:/var/cache/man:/bin/sh
mail:x:8:8:mail:/var/mail:/bin/sh
news:x:9:9:news:/var/spool/news:/bin/sh
```

```
backup:x:34:34:backup:/var/backups:/bin/sh
$
```

Notice that the number 1 is added before the delete edit command. This instructs the sed to perform the editing command on the first line of the file. In this example, the sed will delete the first line of /etc/password and print the rest of the file.

The sed Address Ranges

We will now understand how to work with the sed address ranges. So what if you want to remove more than one line from a file? You can specify an address range with sed as follows —

```
$ cat /etc/passwd | sed '1, 5d' |more
games:x:5:60:games:/usr/games:/bin/sh
man:x:6:12:man:/var/cache/man:/bin/sh
mail:x:8:8:mail:/var/mail:/bin/sh
news:x:9:9:news:/var/spool/news:/bin/sh
backup:x:34:34:backup:/var/backups:/bin/sh
$
```

The above command will be applied on all the lines starting from 1 through 5. This deletes the first five lines.

Try out the following address ranges —

S.No.	Range & Description
1	'4,10d' Lines starting from the 4th till the 10th are deleted

2	'10,4d' Only 10th line is deleted, because the sed does not work in reverse direction
3	'4,+5d' This matches line 4 in the file, deletes that line, continues to delete the next five lines, and then ceases its deletion and prints the rest
4	'2,5!d' This deletes everything except starting from 2nd till 5th line
5	'1~3d' This deletes the first line, steps over the next three lines, and then deletes the fourth line. Sed continues to apply this pattern until the end of the file.

6	'2~2d'
	This tells sed to delete the second line, step over the next line, delete the next line, and repeat until the end of the file is reached
7	'4,10p'
	Lines starting from 4th till 10th are printed
8	'4,d'
	This generates the syntax error
9	',10d'
	This would also generate syntax error

Note — While using the p action, you should use the -n option to avoid repetition of line printing. Check the difference in between the following two commands —

$ cat /etc/passwd | sed -n '1,3p'

Check the above command without -n as follows —

$ cat /etc/passwd | sed '1,3p'

The Substitution Command

The substitution command, denoted by s, will substitute any string that you specify with any other string that you specify.

To substitute one string with another, the sed needs to have the information on where the first string ends and the substitution string begins. For this, we proceed with bookending the two strings with the forward slash (/) character.

The following command substitutes the first occurrence on a line of the string root with the string amrood.

```
$ cat /etc/passwd | sed 's/root/amrood/'
amrood:x:0:0:root user:/root:/bin/sh
daemon:x:1:1:daemon:/usr/sbin:/bin/sh
........................
```

It is very important to note that sed substitutes only the first occurrence on a line. If the string root occurs more than once on a line only the first match will be replaced.

For the sed to perform a global substitution, add the letter g to the end of the command as follows —

```
$ cat /etc/passwd | sed 's/root/amrood/g'
amrood:x:0:0:amrood user:/amrood:/bin/sh
daemon:x:1:1:daemon:/usr/sbin:/bin/sh
bin:x:2:2:bin:/bin:/bin/sh
sys:x:3:3:sys:/dev:/bin/sh
........................
```

Substitution Flags

There are a number of other useful flags that can be passed in addition to the g flag, and you can specify more than one at a time.

S.No.	Flag & Description
1	g Replaces all matches, not just the first match
2	NUMBER Replaces only NUMBERth match
3	p If substitution was made, then prints the pattern space
4	w FILENAME If substitution was made, then writes result to FILENAME
5	I or i Matches in a case-insensitive manner

6	M or m
	In addition to the normal behavior of the special regular expression characters ^ and $, this flag causes ^ to match the empty string after a newline and $ to match the empty string before a newline

Using an Alternative String Separator

Suppose you have to do a substitution on a string that includes the forward slash character. In this case, you can specify a different separator by providing the designated character after the s.

```
$ cat /etc/passwd | sed 's:/root:/amrood:g'
amrood:x:0:0:amrood user:/amrood:/bin/sh
daemon:x:1:1:daemon:/usr/sbin:/bin/sh
```

In the above example, we have used : as the delimiter instead of slash / because we were trying to search /root instead of the simple root.

Replacing with Empty Space

Use an empty substitution string to delete the root string from the /etc/passwd file entirely −

```
$ cat /etc/passwd | sed 's/root//g'
:x:0:0::/:/bin/sh
daemon:x:1:1:daemon:/usr/sbin:/bin/sh
```

Address Substitution

If you want to substitute the string sh with the string quiet only on line 10, you can specify it as follows —

```
$ cat /etc/passwd | sed '10s/sh/quiet/g'
root:x:0:0:root user:/root:/bin/sh
daemon:x:1:1:daemon:/usr/sbin:/bin/sh
bin:x:2:2:bin:/bin:/bin/sh
sys:x:3:3:sys:/dev:/bin/sh
sync:x:4:65534:sync:/bin:/bin/sync
games:x:5:60:games:/usr/games:/bin/sh
man:x:6:12:man:/var/cache/man:/bin/sh
mail:x:8:8:mail:/var/mail:/bin/sh
news:x:9:9:news:/var/spool/news:/bin/sh
backup:x:34:34:backup:/var/backups:/bin/quiet
```

Similarly, to do an address range substitution, you could do something like the following —

```
$ cat /etc/passwd | sed '1,5s/sh/quiet/g'
root:x:0:0:root user:/root:/bin/quiet
daemon:x:1:1:daemon:/usr/sbin:/bin/quiet
bin:x:2:2:bin:/bin:/bin/quiet
sys:x:3:3:sys:/dev:/bin/quiet
sync:x:4:65534:sync:/bin:/bin/sync
games:x:5:60:games:/usr/games:/bin/sh
man:x:6:12:man:/var/cache/man:/bin/sh
mail:x:8:8:mail:/var/mail:/bin/sh
news:x:9:9:news:/var/spool/news:/bin/sh
backup:x:34:34:backup:/var/backups:/bin/sh
```

As you can see from the output, the first five lines had the string sh changed to quiet, but the rest of the lines were left untouched.

The Matching Command

You would use the p option along with the -n option to print all the matching lines as follows −

```
$ cat testing | sed -n '/root/p'
root:x:0:0:root user:/root:/bin/sh
[root@ip-72-167-112-17 amrood]# vi testing
root:x:0:0:root user:/root:/bin/sh
daemon:x:1:1:daemon:/usr/sbin:/bin/sh
bin:x:2:2:bin:/bin:/bin/sh
sys:x:3:3:sys:/dev:/bin/sh
sync:x:4:65534:sync:/bin:/bin/sync
games:x:5:60:games:/usr/games:/bin/sh
man:x:6:12:man:/var/cache/man:/bin/sh
mail:x:8:8:mail:/var/mail:/bin/sh
news:x:9:9:news:/var/spool/news:/bin/sh
backup:x:34:34:backup:/var/backups:/bin/sh
```

Using Regular Expression

While matching patterns, you can use the regular expression which provides more flexibility.

Check the following example which matches all the lines starting with *daemon*and then deletes them −

```
$ cat testing | sed '/^daemon/d'
root:x:0:0:root user:/root:/bin/sh
bin:x:2:2:bin:/bin:/bin/sh
sys:x:3:3:sys:/dev:/bin/sh
sync:x:4:65534:sync:/bin:/bin/sync
games:x:5:60:games:/usr/games:/bin/sh
man:x:6:12:man:/var/cache/man:/bin/sh
mail:x:8:8:mail:/var/mail:/bin/sh
news:x:9:9:news:/var/spool/news:/bin/sh
backup:x:34:34:backup:/var/backups:/bin/sh
```

Following is the example which deletes all the lines ending with sh —

```
$ cat testing | sed '/sh$/d'
sync:x:4:65534:sync:/bin:/bin/sync
```

The following table lists four special characters that are very useful in regular expressions.

S.No.	Character & Description
1	^ Matches the beginning of lines
2	$ Matches the end of lines
3	. Matches any single character
4	* Matches zero or more occurrences of the previous

S.No.	Expression & Description
	character
5	[chars] Matches any one of the characters given in chars, where chars is a sequence of characters. You can use the - character to indicate a range of characters.

Matching Characters

Look at a few more expressions to demonstrate the use of metacharacters. For example, the following pattern —

S.No.	Expression & Description
1	/a.c/ Matches lines that contain strings such as a+c, a-c, abc, match, and a3c
2	/a*c/ Matches the same strings along with strings such as ace, yacc, and arctic

3	/[tT]he/ Matches the string The and the
4	/^$/ Matches blank lines
5	/^.*$/ Matches an entire line whatever it is
6	/ */ Matches one or more spaces
7	/^$/ Matches blank lines

Following table shows some frequently used sets of characters —

S.No.	Set & Description
1	[a-z] Matches a single lowercase letter
2	[A-Z] Matches a single uppercase letter
3	[a-zA-Z] Matches a single letter
4	[0-9] Matches a single number
5	[a-zA-Z0-9] Matches a single letter or number

Character Class Keywords

Some special keywords are commonly available to regexps, especially GNU utilities that employ regexps. These are very useful for sed regular expressions as they simplify things and enhance readability.

For example, the characters a through z and the characters A through Z, constitute one such class of characters that has the keyword [[:alpha:]]

Using the alphabet character class keyword, this command prints only those lines in the /etc/syslog.conf file that start with a letter of the alphabet —

```
$ cat /etc/syslog.conf | sed -n '/^[[:alpha:]]/p'
authpriv.*              /var/log/secure
mail.*                  -/var/log/maillog
cron.*                  /var/log/cron
uucp,news.crit           /var/log/spooler
local7.*                /var/log/boot.log
```

The following table is a complete list of the available character class keywords in GNU sed.

S.No.	Character Class & Description
1	[[:alnum:]] Alphanumeric [a-z A-Z 0-9]

2	[[:alpha:]] Alphabetic [a-z A-Z]
3	[[:blank:]] Blank characters (spaces or tabs)
4	[[:cntrl:]] Control characters
5	[[:digit:]] Numbers [0-9]
6	[[:graph:]] Any visible characters (excludes whitespace)
7	[[:lower:]]

	Lowercase letters [a-z]	
8	[[:print:]] Printable characters (non-control characters)	
9	[[:punct:]] Punctuation characters	
10	[[:space:]] Whitespace	
11	[[:upper:]] Uppercase letters [A-Z]	
12	[[:xdigit:]] Hex digits [0-9 a-f A-F]	

Aampersand Referencing

The sed metacharacter & represents the contents of the pattern that was matched. For instance, say you have a file called phone.txt full of phone numbers, such as the following —

```
5555551212
5555551213
5555551214
6665551215
6665551216
7775551217
```

You want to make the area code (the first three digits) surrounded by parentheses for easier reading. To do this, you can use the ampersand replacement character —

```
$ sed -e 's/^[[:digit:]][[:digit:]][[:digit:]]/(&)/g' phone.txt
(555)5551212
(555)5551213
(555)5551214
(666)5551215

(666)5551216
(777)5551217
```

Here in the pattern part you are matching the first 3 digits and then using &you are replacing those 3 digits with the surrounding parentheses.

Using Multiple sed Commands

You can use multiple sed commands in a single sed command as follows —

```
$ sed -e 'command1' -e 'command2' ... -e 'commandN' files
```

Here command1 through commandN are sed commands of the type discussed previously. These commands are applied to each of the lines in the list of files given by files.

Using the same mechanism, we can write the above phone number example as follows −

```
$ sed -e 's/^[[:digit:]]\{3\}/(&)/g' \
  -e 's/)[[:digit:]]\{3\}/&-/g' phone.txt
(555)555-1212
(555)555-1213
(555)555-1214
(666)555-1215
(666)555-1216
(777)555-1217
```

Note − In the above example, instead of repeating the character class keyword [[:digit:]] three times, we replaced it with \{3\}, which means the preceding regular expression is matched three times. We have also used \ to give line break and this has to be removed before the command is run.

Back References

The ampersand metacharacter is useful, but even more useful is the ability to define specific regions in regular expressions. These special regions can be used as reference in your replacement strings. By defining specific parts of a regular expression, you can then refer back to those parts with a special reference character.

To do back references, you have to first define a region and then refer back to that region. To define a region, you insert backslashed parenthesesaround each region of interest. The first region that you surround with backslashes is then referenced by \1, the second region by \2, and so on.

Assuming phone.txt has the following text –

```
(555)555-1212
(555)555-1213
(555)555-1214
(666)555-1215
(666)555-1216
(777)555-1217
```

Try the following command –

```
$ cat phone.txt | sed 's/\(.*)\)\(.*-\)\(.*$\)/Area \
   code: \1 Second: \2 Third: \3/'
Area code: (555) Second: 555- Third: 1212
Area code: (555) Second: 555- Third: 1213
Area code: (555) Second: 555- Third: 1214
Area code: (666) Second: 555- Third: 1215
Area code: (666) Second: 555- Third: 1216
Area code: (777) Second: 555- Third: 1217
```

Note – In the above example, each regular expression inside the parenthesis would be back referenced by \1, \2 and so on. We have used \ to give line break here. This should be removed before running the command.

Unix - File System Basics

A file system is a logical collection of files on a partition or disk. A partition is a container for information and can span an entire hard drive if desired.

Your hard drive can have various partitions which usually contain only one file system, such as one file system housing the /file system or another containing the /home file system.

One file system per partition allows for the logical maintenance and management of differing file systems.

Everything in Unix is considered to be a file, including physical devices such as DVD-ROMs, USB devices, and floppy drives.

Directory Structure

Unix uses a hierarchical file system structure, much like an upside-down tree, with root (/) at the base of the file system and all other directories spreading from there.

A Unix filesystem is a collection of files and directories that has the following properties —

- It has a root directory (/) that contains other files and directories.
- Each file or directory is uniquely identified by its name, the directory in which it resides, and a unique identifier, typically called an inode.
- By convention, the root directory has an inode number of 2 and the lost+found directory has an inode number of 3. Inode numbers 0and 1 are not used. File inode numbers can be seen by specifying the -i option to ls command.

- It is self-contained. There are no dependencies between one filesystem and another.

The directories have specific purposes and generally hold the same types of information for easily locating files. Following are the directories that exist on the major versions of Unix –

S.No.	Directory & Description
1	/ This is the root directory which should contain only the directories needed at the top level of the file structure
2	/bin This is where the executable files are located. These files are available to all users
3	/dev These are device drivers

4	/etc Supervisor directory commands, configuration files, disk configuration files, valid user lists, groups, ethernet, hosts, where to send critical messages
5	/lib Contains shared library files and sometimes other kernel-related files
6	/boot Contains files for booting the system
7	/home Contains the home directory for users and other accounts

8	/mnt
	Used to mount other temporary file systems, such as cdrom and floppy for the CD-ROM drive and floppy diskette drive, respectively
9	/proc
	Contains all processes marked as a file by process number or other information that is dynamic to the system
10	/tmp
	Holds temporary files used between system boots
11	/usr
	Used for miscellaneous purposes, and can be used by many users. Includes administrative commands, shared files, library files, and others

12	/var
	Typically contains variable-length files such as log and print files and any other type of file that may contain a variable amount of data
13	/sbin
	Contains binary (executable) files, usually for system administration. For example, *fdisk* and *ifconfig* utlities
14	/kernel
	Contains kernel files

Navigating the File System

Now that you understand the basics of the file system, you can begin navigating to the files you need. The following commands are used to navigate the system −

S.No.	Command & Description
1	cat filename

		Displays a filename
2	cd dirname	Moves you to the identified directory
3	cp file1 file2	Copies one file/directory to the specified location
4	file filename	Identifies the file type (binary, text, etc)
5	find filename dir	Finds a file/directory
6	head filename	Shows the beginning of a file

7	less filename
	Browses through a file from the end or the beginning
8	ls dirname
	Shows the contents of the directory specified
9	mkdir dirname
	Creates the specified directory
10	more filename
	Browses through a file from the beginning to the end
11	mv file1 file2
	Moves the location of, or renames a file/directory
12	pwd

	Shows the current directory the user is in	
13	rm filename Removes a file	
14	rmdir dirname Removes a directory	
15	tail filename Shows the end of a file	
16	touch filename Creates a blank file or modifies an existing file or its attributes	
17	whereis filename	

	Shows the location of a file	
18	which filename	
	Shows the location of a file if it is in your PATH	

You can use Manpage Help to check complete syntax for each command mentioned here.

The df Command

The first way to manage your partition space is with the df (disk free)command. The command df -k (disk free) displays the disk space usage in kilobytes, as shown below –

```
$df -k
Filesystem     1K-blocks     Used   Available Use% Mounted on
/dev/vzfs      10485760   7836644    2649116  75% /
/devices              0         0          0   0% /devices
$
```

Some of the directories, such as /devices, shows 0 in the kbytes, used, and avail columns as well as 0% for capacity. These are special (or virtual) file systems, and although they reside on the disk under /, by themselves they do not consume disk space.

The df -k output is generally the same on all Unix systems. Here's what it usually includes –

S.No.	Column & Description
1	Filesystem The physical file system name
2	kbytes Total kilobytes of space available on the storage medium
3	used Total kilobytes of space used (by files)
4	avail Total kilobytes available for use
5	capacity Percentage of total space used by files

6	Mounted on
	What the file system is mounted on

You can use the -h (human readable) option to display the output in a format that shows the size in easier-to-understand notation.

The du Command

The du (disk usage) command enables you to specify directories to show disk space usage on a particular directory.

This command is helpful if you want to determine how much space a particular directory is taking. The following command displays number of blocks consumed by each directory. A single block may take either 512 Bytes or 1 Kilo Byte depending on your system.

```
$du /etc
10    /etc/cron.d
126   /etc/default
6     /etc/dfs
...
$
```

The -h option makes the output easier to comprehend —

```
$du -h /etc
5k    /etc/cron.d
63k   /etc/default
3k    /etc/dfs
...
$
```

Mounting the File System

A file system must be mounted in order to be usable by the system. To see what is currently mounted (available for use) on your system, use the following command —

```
$ mount
/dev/vzfs on / type reiserfs (rw,usrquota,grpquota)
proc on /proc type proc (rw,nodiratime)
devpts on /dev/pts type devpts (rw)
$
```

The /mnt directory, by the Unix convention, is where temporary mounts (such as CDROM drives, remote network drives, and floppy drives) are located. If you need to mount a file system, you can use the mount command with the following syntax —

```
mount -t file_system_type device_to_mount directory_to_mount_to
```

For example, if you want to mount a CD-ROM to the directory /mnt/cdrom, you can type —

```
$ mount -t iso9660 /dev/cdrom /mnt/cdrom
```

This assumes that your CD-ROM device is called /dev/cdrom and that you want to mount it to /mnt/cdrom. Refer to the mount man page for more specific information or type mount -h at the command line for help information.

After mounting, you can use the cd command to navigate the newly available file system through the mount point you just made.

Unmounting the File System

To unmount (remove) the file system from your system, use the umountcommand by identifying the mount point or device.

For example, to unmount cdrom, use the following command −

```
$ umount /dev/cdrom
```

The mount command enables you to access your file systems, but on most modern Unix systems, the automount function makes this process invisible to the user and requires no intervention.

User and Group Quotas

The user and group quotas provide the mechanisms by which the amount of space used by a single user or all users within a specific group can be limited to a value defined by the administrator.

Quotas operate around two limits that allow the user to take some action if the amount of space or number of disk blocks start to exceed the administrator defined limits −

- Soft Limit − If the user exceeds the limit defined, there is a grace period that allows the user to free up some space.
- Hard Limit − When the hard limit is reached, regardless of the grace period, no further files or blocks can be allocated.

There are a number of commands to administer quotas −

S.No.	Command & Description
1	quota Displays disk usage and limits for a user of group
2	edquota This is a quota editor. Users or Groups quota can be edited using this command
3	quotacheck Scans a filesystem for disk usage, creates, checks and repairs quota files
4	setquota This is a command line quota editor

5	quotaon
	This announces to the system that disk quotas should be enabled on one or more filesystems
6	quotaoff
	This announces to the system that disk quotas should be disabled for one or more filesystems
7	repquota
	This prints a summary of the disc usage and quotas for the specified file systems

You can use Manpage Help to check complete syntax for each command mentioned here.

Unix - User Administration

In this chapter, we will discuss in detail about user administration in Unix.

There are three types of accounts on a Unix system —

Root account

This is also called superuser and would have complete and unfettered control of the system. A superuser can run any commands without any restriction. This user should be assumed as a system administrator.

System accounts

System accounts are those needed for the operation of system-specific components for example mail accounts and the sshd accounts. These accounts are usually needed for some specific function on your system, and any modifications to them could adversely affect the system.

User accounts

User accounts provide interactive access to the system for users and groups of users. General users are typically assigned to these accounts and usually have limited access to critical system files and directories.

Unix supports a concept of *Group Account* which logically groups a number of accounts. Every account would be a part of another group account. A Unix group plays important role in handling file permissions and process management.

Managing Users and Groups

There are four main user administration files —

- /etc/passwd — Keeps the user account and password information. This file holds the majority of information about accounts on the Unix system.
- /etc/shadow — Holds the encrypted password of the corresponding account. Not all the systems support this file.
- /etc/group — This file contains the group information for each account.
- /etc/gshadow — This file contains secure group account information.

Check all the above files using the cat command.

The following table lists out commands that are available on majority of Unix systems to create and manage accounts and groups —

S.No.	Command & Description
1	useradd Adds accounts to the system
2	usermod Modifies account attributes

3	userdel
	Deletes accounts from the system
4	groupadd
	Adds groups to the system
5	groupmod
	Modifies group attributes
6	groupdel
	Removes groups from the system

You can use Manpage Help to check complete syntax for each command mentioned here.

Create a Group

We will now understand how to create a group. For this, we need to create groups before creating any account otherwise, we can make use of the existing groups in our system. We have all the groups listed in /etc/groupsfile.

All the default groups are system account specific groups and it is not recommended to use them for ordinary accounts. So, following is the syntax to create a new group account −

groupadd [-g gid [-o]] [-r] [-f] groupname

The following table lists out the parameters −

S.No.	Option & Description
1	-g GID The numerical value of the group's ID
2	-o This option permits to add group with non-unique GID
3	-r This flag instructs groupadd to add a system account

4	-f
	This option causes to just exit with success status, if the specified group already exists. With -g, if the specified GID already exists, other (unique) GID is chosen
5	groupname
	Actual group name to be created

If you do not specify any parameter, then the system makes use of the default values.

Following example creates a *developers* group with default values, which is very much acceptable for most of the administrators.

$ groupadd developers

Modify a Group

To modify a group, use the groupmod syntax –

$ groupmod -n new_modified_group_name old_group_name

To change the developers_2 group name to developer, type −

$ groupmod -n developer developer_2

Here is how you will change the financial GID to 545 −

$ groupmod -g 545 developer

Delete a Group

We will now understand how to delete a group. To delete an existing group, all you need is the groupdel command and the group name. To delete the financial group, the command is −

$ groupdel developer

This removes only the group, not the files associated with that group. The files are still accessible by their owners.

Create an Account

Let us see how to create a new account on your Unix system. Following is the syntax to create a user's account −

useradd -d homedir -g groupname -m -s shell -u userid accountname

The following table lists out the parameters —

S.No.	Option & Description
1	-d homedir Specifies home directory for the account
2	-g groupname Specifies a group account for this account
3	-m Creates the home directory if it doesn't exist
4	-s shell Specifies the default shell for this account
5	-u userid You can specify a user id for this account

6	accountname
	Actual account name to be created

If you do not specify any parameter, then the system makes use of the default values. The useradd command modifies the /etc/passwd, /etc/shadow, and /etc/group files and creates a home directory.

Following is the example that creates an account *mcmohd*, setting its home directory to */home/mcmohd* and the group as *developers*. This user would have Korn Shell assigned to it.

```
$ useradd -d /home/mcmohd -g developers -s /bin/ksh mcmohd
```

Before issuing the above command, make sure you already have the *developers* group created using the *groupadd* command.

Once an account is created you can set its password using the passwdcommand as follows −

```
$ passwd mcmohd20
Changing password for user mcmohd20.
New UNIX password:
Retype new UNIX password:
passwd: all authentication tokens updated successfully.
```

When you type *passwd accountname*, it gives you an option to change the password, provided you are a superuser. Otherwise, you can change just your password using the same command but without specifying your account name.

Modify an Account

The usermod command enables you to make changes to an existing account from the command line. It uses the same arguments as the useraddcommand, plus the -l argument, which allows you to change the account name.

For example, to change the account name *mcmohd* to *mcmohd20* and to change home directory accordingly, you will need to issue the following command —

$ usermod -d /home/mcmohd20 -m -l mcmohd mcmohd20

Delete an Account

The userdel command can be used to delete an existing user. This is a very dangerous command if not used with caution.

There is only one argument or option available for the command .r, for removing the account's home directory and mail file.

For example, to remove account *mcmohd20*, issue the following command —

$ userdel -r mcmohd20

If you want to keep the home directory for backup purposes, omit the -roption. You can remove the home directory as needed at a later time.

Unix - System Performance

In this chapter, we will discuss in detail about the system performance in Unix.

We will introduce you to a few free tools that are available to monitor and manage performance on Unix systems. These tools also provide guidelines on how to diagnose and fix performance problems in the Unix environment.

Unix has following major resource types that need to be monitored and tuned —

- CPU
- Memory
- Disk space
- Communications lines
- I/O Time
- Network Time
- Applications programs

Performance Components

The following table lists out five major components which take up the system time —

S.No.	Component & Description
1	**User State CPU** The actual amount of time the CPU spends running the users' program in the user state. It includes the time spent executing library calls, but does not include the time spent in the kernel on its behalf
2	**System State CPU** This is the amount of time the CPU spends in the system state on behalf of this program. All I/O routines require kernel services. The programmer can affect this value by blocking I/O transfers
3	**I/O Time and Network Time** This is the amount of time spent moving data and servicing I/O requests

4	Virtual Memory Performance
	This includes context switching and swapping
5	Application Program
	Time spent running other programs - when the system is not servicing this application because another application currently has the CPU

Performance Tools

Unix provides following important tools to measure and fine tune Unix system performance –

S.No.	Command & Description
1	nice/renice
	Runs a program with modified scheduling priority

2	netstat
	Prints network connections, routing tables, interface statistics, masquerade connections, and multicast memberships
3	time
	Helps time a simple command or give resource usage
4	uptime
	This is System Load Average
5	ps
	Reports a snapshot of the current processes
6	vmstat
	Reports virtual memory statistics

7	gprof
	Displays call graph profile data
8	prof
	Facilitates Process Profiling
9	top
	Displays system tasks

You can use Manpage Help to check complete syntax for each command mentioned here.

Unix - System Logging

In this chapter, we will discuss in detail about system logging in Unix.

Unix systems have a very flexible and powerful logging system, which enables you to record almost anything you can imagine and then manipulate the logs to retrieve the information you require.

Many versions of Unix provide a general-purpose logging facility called syslog. Individual programs that need to have information logged, send the information to syslog.

Unix *syslog* is a host-configurable, uniform system logging facility. The system uses a centralized system logging process that runs the program /etc/syslogd or /etc/syslog.

The operation of the system logger is quite straightforward. Programs send their log entries to *syslogd*, which consults the configuration file /etc/syslogd.conf or /etc/syslog and, when a match is found, writes the log message to the desired log file.

There are four basic syslog terms that you should understand —

S.No.	Term & Description
1	Facility The identifier used to describe the application or process that submitted the log message. For

example, mail, kernel, and ftp.

2	Priority
	An indicator of the importance of the message. Levels are defined within syslog as guidelines, from debugging information to critical events.

3	Selector
	A combination of one or more facilities and levels. When an incoming event matches a selector, an action is performed.

4	Action
	What happens to an incoming message that matches a selector — Actions can write the message to a log file, echo the message to a console or other device, write the message to a logged in user, or send the message along to another syslog server.

Syslog Facilities

We will now understand about the syslog facilities. Here are the available facilities for the selector. Not all facilities are present on all versions of Unix.

Facility	Description
1	auth Activity related to requesting name and password (getty, su, login)
2	authpriv Same as auth but logged to a file that can only be read by selected users
3	console Used to capture messages that are generally directed to the system console
4	cron

	Messages from the cron system scheduler	
5	daemon	
	System daemon catch-all	
6	ftp	
	Messages relating to the ftp daemon	
7	kern	
	Kernel messages	
8	local0.local7	
	Local facilities defined per site	
9	lpr	
	Messages from the line printing system	

10	mail
	Messages relating to the mail system
11	mark
	Pseudo-event used to generate timestamps in log files
12	news
	Messages relating to network news protocol (nntp)
13	ntp
	Messages relating to network time protocol
14	user
	Regular user processes

15	uucp
	UUCP subsystem

Syslog Priorities

The syslog priorities are summarized in the following table —

S.No.	Priority & Description
1	emerg Emergency condition, such as an imminent system crash, usually broadcast to all users
2	alert Condition that should be corrected immediately, such as a corrupted system database
3	crit Critical condition, such as a hardware error

4	err
	Ordinary error
5	Warning
	Warning
6	notice
	Condition that is not an error, but possibly should be handled in a special way
7	info
	Informational message
8	debug
	Messages that are used when debugging programs

9	none
	Pseudo level used to specify not to log messages

The combination of facilities and levels enables you to be discerning about what is logged and where that information goes.

As each program sends its messages dutifully to the system logger, the logger makes decisions on what to keep track of and what to discard based on the levels defined in the selector.

When you specify a level, the system will keep track of everything at that level and higher.

The /etc/syslog.conf file

The /etc/syslog.conf file controls where messages are logged. A typical syslog.conf file might look like this —

```
*.err;kern.debug;auth.notice /dev/console
daemon,auth.notice      /var/log/messages
lpr.info              /var/log/lpr.log
mail.*               /var/log/mail.log
ftp.*                /var/log/ftp.log
auth.*                @prep.ai.mit.edu
auth.*                root,amrood
netinfo.err           /var/log/netinfo.log
install.*             /var/log/install.log
*.emerg               *
*.alert               |program_name
mark.*                /dev/console
```

Each line of the file contains two parts —

- A message selector that specifies which kind of messages to log. For example, all error messages or all debugging messages from the kernel.
- An action field that says what should be done with the message. For example, put it in a file or send the message to a user's terminal.

Following are the notable points for the above configuration —

- Message selectors have two parts: a facility and a priority. For example, *kern.debug* selects all debug messages (the priority) generated by the kernel (the facility).
- Message selector *kern.debug* selects all priorities that are greater than debug.
- An asterisk in place of either the facility or the priority indicates "all". For example, *.debug means all debug messages, while kern.*means all messages generated by the kernel.
- You can also use commas to specify multiple facilities. Two or more selectors can be grouped together by using a semicolon.

Logging Actions

The action field specifies one of five actions —

- Log message to a file or a device. For example, /var/log/lpr.log or /dev/console.
- Send a message to a user. You can specify multiple usernames by separating them with commas; for example, root, amrood.
- Send a message to all users. In this case, the action field consists of an asterisk; for example, *.

- Pipe the message to a program. In this case, the program is specified after the Unix pipe symbol (|).
- Send the message to the syslog on another host. In this case, the action field consists of a hostname, preceded by an at sign; for example, @markanthony.com

The logger Command

Unix provides the logger command, which is an extremely useful command to deal with system logging. The logger command sends logging messages to the syslogd daemon, and consequently provokes system logging.

This means we can check from the command line at any time the syslogddaemon and its configuration. The logger command provides a method for adding one-line entries to the system log file from the command line.

The format of the command is −

logger [-i] [-f file] [-p priority] [-t tag] [message]...

Here is the detail of the parameters −

S.No.	Option & Description
1	-f filename Uses the contents of file filename as the message to log.

2	-i
	Logs the process ID of the logger process with each line.
3	-p priority
	Enters the message with the specified priority (specified selector entry); the message priority can be specified numerically, or as a facility.priority pair. The default priority is user.notice.
4	-t tag
	Marks each line added to the log with the specified tag.
5	message
	The string arguments whose contents are concatenated together in the specified order, separated by the space.

You can use Manpage Help to check complete syntax for this command.

Log Rotation

Log files have the propensity to grow very fast and consume large amounts of disk space. To enable log rotations, most distributions use tools such as *newsyslog* or *logrotate*.

These tools should be called on a frequent time interval using the cron daemon. Check the man pages for *newsyslog* or *logrotate* for more details.

Important Log Locations

All the system applications create their log files in */var/log* and its sub-directories. Here are few important applications and their corresponding log directories −

Application	Directory
httpd	/var/log/httpd
samba	/var/log/samba
cron	/var/log/
mail	/var/log/
mysql	/var/log/

Unix - Signals and Traps

In this chapter, we will discuss in detail about Signals and Traps in Unix.

Signals are software interrupts sent to a program to indicate that an important event has occurred. The events can vary from user requests to illegal memory access errors. Some signals, such as the interrupt signal, indicate that a user has asked the program to do something that is not in the usual flow of control.

The following table lists out common signals you might encounter and want to use in your programs —

Signal Name	Signal Number	Description
SIGHUP	1	Hang up detected on controlling terminal or death of controlling process
SIGINT	2	Issued if the user sends an interrupt signal (Ctrl + C)
SIGQUIT	3	Issued if the user sends a quit signal (Ctrl + D)

SIGFPE	8	Issued if an illegal mathematical operation is attempted
SIGKILL	9	If a process gets this signal it must quit immediately and will not perform any clean-up operations
SIGALRM	14	Alarm clock signal (used for timers)
SIGTERM	15	Software termination signal (sent by kill by default)

List of Signals

There is an easy way to list down all the signals supported by your system. Just issue the kill -l command and it would display all the supported signals —

```
$ kill -l
 1) SIGHUP      2) SIGINT     3) SIGQUIT    4) SIGILL
 5) SIGTRAP     6) SIGABRT    7) SIGBUS     8) SIGFPE
 9) SIGKILL    10) SIGUSR1   11) SIGSEGV   12) SIGUSR2
13) SIGPIPE    14) SIGALRM   15) SIGTERM   16) SIGSTKFLT
17) SIGCHLD    18) SIGCONT   19) SIGSTOP   20) SIGTSTP
21) SIGTTIN    22) SIGTTOU   23) SIGURG    24) SIGXCPU
25) SIGXFSZ    26) SIGVTALRM 27) SIGPROF   28) SIGWINCH
29) SIGIO      30) SIGPWR    31) SIGSYS    34) SIGRTMIN
35) SIGRTMIN+1 36) SIGRTMIN+2 37) SIGRTMIN+3 38) SIGRTMIN+4
39) SIGRTMIN+5 40) SIGRTMIN+6 41) SIGRTMIN+7 42) SIGRTMIN+8
43) SIGRTMIN+9 44) SIGRTMIN+10 45) SIGRTMIN+11 46) SIGRTMIN+12
47) SIGRTMIN+13 48) SIGRTMIN+14 49) SIGRTMIN+15 50) SIGRTMAX-14
51) SIGRTMAX-13 52) SIGRTMAX-12 53) SIGRTMAX-11 54) SIGRTMAX-10
55) SIGRTMAX-9 56) SIGRTMAX-8 57) SIGRTMAX-7 58) SIGRTMAX-6
```

59) SIGRTMAX-5 60) SIGRTMAX-4 61) SIGRTMAX-3 62) SIGRTMAX-2
63) SIGRTMAX-1 64) SIGRTMAX

The actual list of signals varies between Solaris, HP-UX, and Linux.

Default Actions

Every signal has a default action associated with it. The default action for a signal is the action that a script or program performs when it receives a signal.

Some of the possible default actions are −

- Terminate the process.
- Ignore the signal.
- Dump core. This creates a file called core containing the memory image of the process when it received the signal.
- Stop the process.
- Continue a stopped process.

Sending Signals

There are several methods of delivering signals to a program or script. One of the most common is for a user to type CONTROL-C or the INTERRUPT keywhile a script is executing.

When you press the *Ctrl+C* key, a SIGINT is sent to the script and as per defined default action script terminates.

The other common method for delivering signals is to use the kill command, the syntax of which is as follows −

```
$ kill -signal pid
```

Here signal is either the number or name of the signal to deliver and pid is the process ID that the signal should be sent to. For Example —

$ kill -1 1001

The above command sends the HUP or hang-up signal to the program that is running with process ID 1001. To send a kill signal to the same process, use the following command —

$ kill -9 1001

This kills the process running with process ID 1001.

Trapping Signals

When you press the *Ctrl+C* or Break key at your terminal during execution of a shell program, normally that program is immediately terminated, and your command prompt returns. This may not always be desirable. For instance, you may end up leaving a bunch of temporary files that won't get cleaned up.

Trapping these signals is quite easy, and the trap command has the following syntax —

$ trap commands signals

Here *command* can be any valid Unix command, or even a user-defined function, and signal can be a list of any number of signals you want to trap.

There are two common uses for trap in shell scripts —

- Clean up temporary files
- Ignore signals

Cleaning Up Temporary Files

As an example of the trap command, the following shows how you can remove some files and then exit if someone tries to abort the program from the terminal —

```
$ trap "rm -f $WORKDIR/work1$$ $WORKDIR/dataout$$; exit" 2
```

From the point in the shell program that this trap is executed, the two files *work1$$* and *dataout$$* will be automatically removed if signal number 2 is received by the program.

Hence, if the user interrupts the execution of the program after this trap is executed, you can be assured that these two files will be cleaned up. The exitcommand that follows the rm is necessary because without it, the execution would continue in the program at the point that it left off when the signal was received.

Signal number 1 is generated for hangup. Either someone intentionally hangs up the line or the line gets accidentally disconnected.

You can modify the preceding trap to also remove the two specified files in this case by adding signal number 1 to the list of signals —

```
$ trap "rm $WORKDIR/work1$$ $WORKDIR/dataout$$; exit" 1 2
```

Now these files will be removed if the line gets hung up or if the *Ctrl+C* key gets pressed.

The commands specified to trap must be enclosed in quotes, if they contain more than one command. Also note that the shell scans the command line at the time that the trap command gets executed and also when one of the listed signals is received.

Thus, in the preceding example, the value of WORKDIR and $$ will be substituted at the time that the trap command is executed. If you wanted this substitution to occur at the time that either signal 1 or 2 was received, you can put the commands inside single quotes —

```
$ trap 'rm $WORKDIR/work1$$ $WORKDIR/dataout$$; exit' 1 2
```

Ignoring Signals

If the command listed for trap is null, the specified signal will be ignored when received. For example, the command —

```
$ trap " 2
```

This specifies that the interrupt signal is to be ignored. You might want to ignore certain signals when performing an operation that you don't want to be interrupted. You can specify multiple signals to be ignored as follows —

```
$ trap " 1 2 3 15
```

Note that the first argument must be specified for a signal to be ignored and is not equivalent to writing the following, which has a separate meaning of its own —

```
$ trap 2
```

If you ignore a signal, all subshells also ignore that signal. However, if you specify an action to be taken on the receipt of a signal, all subshells will still take the default action on receipt of that signal.

Resetting Traps

After you've changed the default action to be taken on receipt of a signal, you can change it back again with the trap if you simply omit the first argument; so —

```
$ trap 1 2
```

This resets the action to be taken on the receipt of signals 1 or 2 back to the default.